JANE WILSON

ON WING
AND WATER

THE LIFE OF LESLIE R COLQUHOUN, DFM, GM, DFC,
WAR HERO, TEST PILOT & HOVERCRAFT PIONEER

JANE WILSON

ON WING
AND WATER

THE LIFE OF LESLIE R COLQUHOUN, DFM, GM, DFC,
WAR HERO, TEST PILOT & HOVERCRAFT PIONEER

MEREO
Cirencester

Mereo Books

1A The Wool Market Dyer Street Cirencester Gloucestershire GL7 2PR
An imprint of Memoirs Publishing www.mereobooks.com

On wing and water: 978-1-86151-358-8

First published in Great Britain in 2014
by Mereo Books, an imprint of Memoirs Publishing

Copyright ©2014

The address for Memoirs Publishing Group Limited can be found at
www.memoirspublishing.com

The Memoirs Publishing Group Ltd Reg. No. 7834348

The Memoirs Publishing Group supports both The Forest Stewardship Council® (FSC®) and
the PEFC® leading international forest-certification organisations. Our books carrying both the
FSC label and the PEFC® and are printed on FSC®-certified paper. FSC® is the only
forest-certification scheme supported by the leading environmental organisations including
Greenpeace. Our paper procurement policy can be found at
www.memoirspublishing.com/environment

Typeset by Wiltshire Associates Publisher Services Ltd. Printed and bound in Great Britain by
Marston Book Services Limited, Oxfordshire

CONTENTS

Introduction

DEDICATION

This book is dedicated to my father's grandchildren, who were a big part of his life and the reason I started to put the book together: Victoria, Charlotte, Rupert, Simon, Oliver, Harriet, Edward, Alexander and Elspeth

ACKNOWLEDGEMENTS

I would like to mention the following books which refer to
my father and were points of reference:

Fly High Fly Low, by Eric B Morgan, a biography of
Leslie written after he died.

Never a Dull Moment, by Denis Le P Webb
(Leslie wrote the foreword)

Into the Jet Age, Chilbolton Airfield 1945 -1962,
by Eleanor M Lockyear.

On a Cushion of Air, by Robin Paine and Roger Syms
(former hovercraft pilots). Robin borrowed photographs
and memorabilia when writing this book.

INTRODUCTION

My father, Leslie Colquhoun, died in April 2001, but it was not until ten years later, when my mother died, that I found a number of talks he had written, plus what I think must have been the start of an autobiography. We all knew that during his latter years he frequently visited various organisations giving talks about various aspects of his life. He had a very interesting career, achieving more things than many of his contemporaries, all with a certain amount of risk. I have attempted to put that life into some sort of chronological order through the talks and articles that were written by him and about him.

Following my father's death, Eric Morgan did write a biography, *Fly High, Fly Low*, but it is very much a technical book and little of my father's true character was revealed. It was written with very little input from my mother, apart from the loan of a number of photographs.

This book recounts every flight that my father made and the duration, such is the detail. Leslie Colquhoun was a very modest, gentle man who loved his work and family. As children there were periods when we did not see a lot of him, but we always knew he was a little different. This did not alter the fact that he was loved and we were very proud of him. We were not aware, as perhaps our mother was, of the danger he faced daily whilst flying. His life was mostly exciting, glamorous and very busy. Among early memories are flying trips over Chilbolton and the airfield in an Auster and freewheeling in the Morris Minor on our way back from Andover!

Leslie Colquhoun was born on 15th March 1921, the elder of Frank and Edith Colquhoun's two children. His sister Edna was born in March 1923. The family home was in Ealing, west London. Leslie's childhood was typical of the time. He was educated locally, ending his schooldays at Drayton Manor School.

The following is an extract from a piece he wrote about his early life:

I suppose that leaving school is the first milestone in the process of growing up. It certainly was for me, suddenly the safe cosy atmosphere of school life was changed to the reality of finding work and in 1936/37 that was not easy. My examination marks excluded me from taking the soft option of applying to join the Civil Service and certainly did not warrant any idea of university life, not that my parents could have afforded the latter. However, one of my many job applications proved successful and I joined W H Cullen, an upmarket grocery and provision chain with some 100-150 branches in the London, Kent and Surrey areas. My job was a junior clerk in their head office near Liverpool Street in London.

Cullen's was an old family business and the old offices and warehouse were almost Dickensian. My first task was sitting on a high stool with a sloping desk adding up countless rows of figures. No computers or adding machines in those days, it all had to be done the hard way, and I must confess that I was not very good at it. However, I soon learned and the mistakes appeared less frequently. I still have the technique, but regrettably the speed and accuracy has dropped a little. Despite the low pay I have happy recollections of working there and I built up an understanding of the complexity of supplying the public with the basic necessities of life.

Working took up a great deal of the day, leaving home at 7.30 a.m. and not getting home until 7.00 in the evening. The long days did not leave much time for leisure activities and in any case even though I was a working teenager I was not allowed to be out after 10.00 p.m. Reading, therefore was a major source of relaxation and it gave me great pleasure. I did meet my friends on Saturdays at their homes or the milk bars that were popular in those days. Drinking and going to pubs were strictly taboo and was not affordable on the wages that we were paid. Landlords were very strict regarding under-age drinking and the off licences, the only other source of supply, would not sell drink to people under the age of 18. However, life was not dull and I can recollect many enjoyable times in those days.

CHAPTER ONE

THE THREAT OF WAR

In 1938 the threat of war with Germany began to grow, and a great deal of our leisure time was taken up talking about the danger and trying to understand what we were going to do about it. When Chamberlain came back from Munich with his promise from Hitler that there would be no war, the sense of relief was tremendous, and he was greeted with great cheers as the saviour of Britain. But the euphoria was not to last, and now with hindsight one can understand that all Chamberlain achieved was a delay which gave Britain a chance to prepare for war.

During that year of so-called peace the process of rearming the British Army, Air Force and the Navy went ahead with gathering speed. Perhaps more importantly, it allowed time for completion of the radar chain established around the south and east coasts of the country to locate and track incoming enemy aircraft at up to 50 miles away, and trial runs to prove its effectiveness. This was to prove invaluable during the Battle of Britain; without it, it is doubtful that the battle could have been won.

Production of Spitfire and Hurricane fighter aircraft was made an urgent priority, and slowly but surely the front-line RAF squadrons began to get their new aircraft and to start training to find their most effective use. The Hurricane and Spitfire were a tremendous advance on any previous type of fighter plane in the RAF. They were faster, more manoeuvrable and able to operate at greater heights than the old biplanes such as the Hawker Fury and Gloster Gladiator. Yet in this respect the Germans had the advantage, since they had already used their Me109s and Junker bombers in the Spanish Civil war in 1936-37.

Through the latter part of 1938 and the beginning of 1939, most people realised that war with Germany was inevitable. Despite his promises to Chamberlain, Hitler gave no sign that he was going to keep his word. Quite the reverse; in March 1939 he invaded Czechoslovakia and began to show his intentions of invading Poland. France and Great Britain responded by saying that if that occurred, they would be prepared to go to war with Germany. However, this long delay in realising the true intentions of Germany lost Britain and France the support of Russia, and in the meantime Hitler signed an agreement with Russia that they would divide

Poland between them, thus avoiding the possibility of the Russians opening an Eastern front against Germany.

Ominously for the citizens of Great Britain, gas masks began to be issued and bomb shelters were being dug. Volunteers were joining up to serve in the Army, Navy and the Air Force and arrangements for conscription were being passed through Parliament. There could be no doubt that Britain was on a war footing.

On the 1st September 1939 German troops entered Poland and an ultimatum was sent to Germany at 9.30 that evening asking them to withdraw. This was not heeded by the Germans and a final ultimatum was sent at 9.00 a.m. on 3rd September stating that if Germany did not withdraw from Poland, Britain would be at war with Germany. France was associated with these ultimatums. At 11.15 that morning, the Prime Minister, Neville Chamberlain, made his dramatic broadcast to the nation stating that Great Britain and France were at war with Germany. His broadcast had hardly ended when the first sirens were heard and everybody rushed for the air raid shelters, fearing the worst. Some 10 minutes later the all-clear was sounded. People emerged from their places of refuge uncertain and puzzled, but very aware that the war had started.

At that particular time I was at the local hospital along with many others, filling sandbags to be used to protect the hospital from bomb blast. When the sirens went, we all stopped work and gradually began to drift towards the bomb shelters. There was no panic, just a realisation that it was the best thing to do. When the all-clear was sounded we emerged from the shelters, all discussing what might have happened but very relieved that there had been no bombing, at least in our area. If this had one result, it was that we continued our work with greater urgency and purpose.

To some extent there was a feeling of anti-climax, and over the last months of 1939 and the earlier months of 1940 there was no real involvement in ground fighting or in the air. However, the threat from German U-boats became very apparent. On the evening of 3rd September the liner Athenia was torpedoed off the north coast of Ireland with the loss of 112 people, some of whom were Americans going home to avoid involvement in the war. Three days later three more ships were sunk near the coast of Spain. Perhaps the biggest disaster was the sinking of the Royal Oak, one of the Navy's biggest battleships, in Scapa Flow, which had been presumed a safe haven for the Fleet. This sinking was carried out by a German U-boat, which got away after the attack. 786 Navy personnel were lost in this disaster.

On the continent Poland was fighting a losing battle against the Germans, while the Russians had annexed the Baltic States of Estonia and Lithuania and were preparing to attack Finland. Our own troops were being shipped into France and Belgium to take up their defensive positions, while to the south the French were manning the Maginot Line, considered impregnable by the French.

Although there were a few sporadic German air raids around the Firth of Forth, the Orkneys and down the east coast of England, it all seemed strangely quiet to the people of England. Life was however changing. The towns and cities were blacked out, long-distance rail travel was disrupted by the troop trains, anti-aircraft guns were appearing around large towns and cities and over London and other vital areas defence barrage balloons floated limply overhead.

The LDV (Local Defence Volunteers), later to become known as the Home Guard, was formed. The recruits were men who were over or under the normal age to join the forces. Their function was to carry out patrols to capture any parachutists or other enemy forces infiltrating the defences. When I joined for a short period prior to joining the RAF they still had not been issued with guns or any uniform. Our main armament was a pick-axe handle. It was as Dad's Army depicted it, serious intent but good fun and comradeship. Everybody realised that Britain faced a real crisis and everybody wanted to help in any way possible.

Spirits were uplifted in December when the Navy succeeded in sinking the Graf Spee, a German pocket battleship, in the mouth of the River Plate in Argentina. This was a major success and not only boosted British morale but was a serious blow for Hitler. The Graf Spee was one of his latest battleships and it had been wreaking havoc in the shipping lanes of the South Atlantic.

However, the overall situation looked bleak. Russia, although temporarily held up by the winter weather in Finland, would undoubtedly overrun that country when the spring thaw started. There was also a problem with Norway and Sweden. Sweden had declared her neutrality, but nevertheless was supplying vital iron ore and steel to Germany. German shipping, including naval ships, was also using the Baltic Sea to return to safe ports in East Germany. In addition, during the winter months when the Bothnia Sea was frozen, Swedish iron ore was being taken overland to Narvik in Norway for shipment to Germany.

Britain and France agreed plans to lay mines in the sea lanes off the Norwegian coast to blockade the ports and also to send troops to Narvik and Trondheim to seize control of the iron ore supplies through Narvik. Both of these operations were difficult, requiring a heavy commitment from the British Navy to protect the convoys of troops and equipment during the long sea passage from the English ports to Norway. Into this tricky situation the Altmark, an auxiliary vessel that had been used to keep the Graf Spee supplied in the South Atlantic before it had been sunk, appeared in Norwegian waters, having eluded all efforts by the British Navy to find her on her voyage back from South America. A British destroyer intercepted the Altmark and forced her to seek refuge in the Josing Fiord. The British destroyer was authorised to enter the fiord, which was in effect a violation of Norway's territorial rights, and board and search the Altmark. Despite the attempts of two Norwegian gunboats to stop this, the Altmark was boarded and searched. In the holds were some 300 British prisoners of war, mainly merchant seaman captured by the Graf Spee.

This incident was a further triumph for the British Navy. However it was to have repercussions, as Hitler, enraged by the news and the danger of Norway coming under British influence, decided that Norway was to be invaded forthwith, and on 1st March 1940 German troops marched into the country. This made the plans for a British landing at Narvik and Trondheim extremely difficult, and although bridgeheads were established north and south of Trondheim and at Narvik, the strong German presence made them untenable and the troops were withdrawn. The King and Queen of Norway were also taken off and sent back to England. The withdrawal was made at severe cost in terms of men, equipment and naval losses, the most serious of which was the sinking of the aircraft carrier Glorious.

When orders for the evacuation were received the pilots opted for an attempt to land back on the carrier, despite the fact that their aircraft were not equipped for such an operation. That they succeeded in doing this was due in no small measure to their skill as pilots and to the co-operation of the crew of the Glorious in steaming the carrier at full speed into the wind, thus reducing the deck speed when the aircraft landed. The tragedy was that within hours of this highly successful operation the *Glorious* was sunk and all the aircraft and most of the crew were lost.

Meanwhile the Germans had launched their offensive against Holland and Belgium. Using the Blitzkrieg tactics which they had perfected in the Spanish Civil War and against Poland, these countries were quickly overrun and the Germans were able to start their push through the gap between the northern limit of the French defensive fortifications of the Maginot Line and the North Sea coastline.

Despite the gallant efforts of the French and British Armies and the RAF and Navy the great retreat began, and on 28th May it was decided that the British Army and remnants of the Belgian and French armies should be evacuated from the beaches of Dunkirk. This evacuation lasted from 28th May until 4th June and during that period some 340,000 troops were transported from the beaches to ports along the south coast of Britain. Some 861 ships from small pleasure craft to destroyers and cruisers from the Royal Navy were involved. RAF fighters covered the beaches and kept the German bombers and fighters from attacking the troops. Thankfully the weather was fine and calm, so that small boats were able to play their part in the operation. 243 ships of all sizes were sunk and many others were damaged.

It was miraculous that so many troops were safely brought back to Britain, but nevertheless it was a stunning setback. When the French surrendered to the Germans within six weeks it was even more catastrophic, and Britain was left standing alone against the might of the German Army and Air Force.

Just prior to the Dunkirk evacuation Mr Chamberlain resigned, and Winston Churchill took over and formed a coalition government. Churchill was a totally different character from Chamberlain. Throughout the thirties Churchill had constantly warned the government against the German threat. Had his pleas for rearmament in the mid-thirties been carried out, Britain and France would have been better prepared for the war that was to come in 1939. Indeed it is conceivable that Hitler might not have embarked on his crusade to conquer Europe. However, Churchill now had a mammoth task. Hitler had total control of Europe and the fate of Great Britain seemed hopeless. But Churchill was a great leader, and as far as he was concerned he would continue the struggle against Hitler to the very end. An extract from his speech to the House of Commons on June 4th gave a clear intention of his will to win:

"We shall fight on the beaches, we shall fight on the landing grounds, we shall fight in the fields and in the streets, we shall fight in the hills; we shall never surrender; and even if, which I do not for a moment believe, this island or a large part of it was subjugated and starving, then our Empire beyond the seas, armed and guarded by the British Fleet, would carry on the struggle, until in God's good time the New World, with all its power and might, steps forth to the rescue and the liberation of the Old." Britain suddenly had a new and inspiring leader.

Hitler did indeed offer terms to conclude the fighting, but these were not acceptable. In fact they were given very short shrift by Churchill and the Government. With the new mood in the country, the emphasis was to re-equip the army and restore morale. This meant that the armament factories had to step up their production to levels previously thought unattainable. Since conscription and recruitment into the armed forces was gathering pace women were asked to work in the factories and take over jobs normally done by men. The LDV took on a new significance. They were issued with rifles, and were now called The Home Guard. Thus everybody was involved and doing what they could to help.

For my part, I volunteered to join the RAF as aircrew. This was in July 1940, just as the German Air Force started to increase the raids on shipping round the coast of England and on some coastal towns. I was fortunate, and was selected for pilot duties and reported for duty in September 1940. This was at the height of the Battle of Britain.

CHAPTER TWO

JOINING THE RAF

After two interviews I was sent to the RAF reception centre at Blackpool. I was given a uniform and began my initial training, which mainly consisted of parade ground drill. We were given a hard time and made to learn that orders were to be obeyed smartly.

The weekend before I went to Blackpool I went to London with some friends to celebrate my last night as a civilian. We went to a show at the London Palladium. During the show the air raid siren was sounded, and as was the custom the audience was told that if we wished we could continue watching the show, but if anybody wanted to leave they could do so. We decided to stay, but towards the end of the show we could hear the anti-aircraft guns firing.

When we left the theatre at the end of the performance, we could hear the guns and see the searchlights. Over to the east there was a huge red glow in the sky. We started to walk towards the glow. As we got to London Bridge we could see that this was caused by huge fires burning the dock areas below Tower Bridge. The noise of guns and bombs falling was both exciting and frightening. The police and air raid wardens stopped us from getting any nearer so we started to go home, but found that the tube trains were not running, and we proceeded to walk to Hammersmith. That was my first experience of bombing. It was in fact the start of the German Air Force's campaign of bombing London. Previously they had concentrated raids on the airfields.

Blackpool was a safe haven away from the bombs of London. The drilling went on for four or five weeks, after which we were posted to an initial Training Wing at Torquay in South West England, and in peacetime a beautiful holiday resort. We started all our ground training as under training pilots, navigation, airmanship and elementary engineering principles were the prime subjects with plenty of drill and physical training as well.

The hotel where we stayed had no creature comforts. We had about four to six men per room depending on its size and we were responsible for making our beds and keeping the room tidy. An inspection was carried out every morning prior to marching to the classrooms. The hotel was at the top of a steep hill and the classrooms were at the bottom, a distance of about a mile and a half. The lectures and drills taking place at the hotel were so arranged that we had to go up and down the hill at least five times a day. By the time I had completed the course, lasting six weeks, I not only knew a lot about navigation and airmanship but I was very fit as well!

The next stage was the elementary flying training. I did the course at Fairoaks near Woking. It lasted about eight weeks and the flying was done in a Tiger Moth. It was quite a strange experience going up in a little aeroplane for the first time. The Tiger Moth is a biplane with two cockpits, one for the pupil and one for the instructor. The cockpits were open, so it was necessary to have special clothing in order to keep warm. We had a Sidcot suit, which was a windproof all-in-one overall type garment, a leather helmet and goggles, leather gauntlets with silk gloves to go inside the gauntlets and sheepskin lined leather flying boots. Later we were issued with leather wool-lined bomber-type jackets. Regrettably I either lost, gave away or otherwise disposed of this gear during the four years I was in the Air Force. Had I kept it, it would have been very valuable now.

After an average of 10-12 hours dual instruction, the trainee pilots were sent off solo. This was a nerve-racking moment, to be on your own with no instructor to correct your mistakes. Going solo was a major step forward in the career of a trained pilot, and there were several who did not reach this standard.

Once confidence had been gained in flying solo, the training became more advanced. Cross-country flying, spinning and forced landings had to be learnt and carried out to the satisfaction of the instructor before one could proceed to the next stage of training, which the was Flying Training School. I went to No 9 FTS at Hullavington, where I flew Masters and Hurricanes. The Master was a single-engined low wing monoplane with two seats in tandem, the rear one for the instructor. It was a much bigger and more powerful aeroplane than the Tiger Moth, especially designed and built to train fighter pilots.

As with the Tiger Moth, after several hours of dual instruction we were sent solo, and it was a proud moment to take off and land this powerful aircraft without the assistance of the instructor. At FTS we were taught practically everything about flying: stalling, spinning, forced landings, formation flying, basic aerial combat, pilot navigation and limited night flying. As an introduction to a real fighter aircraft, we were allowed to do some flying in the Hurricane aircraft. This was the fighter that shared the honours with the Spitfire in the Battle of Britain.

At the end of the FTS course, successful students were presented with their RAF wings at a ceremonial parade. This was the proud moment that made the previous eight months' training and hard work all worthwhile. However, to ensure that we didn't get too over-confident in our flying ability, there was a further training course to be endured before being posted to a

Squadron. This was the Operational Training Unit. Here the instructors were all experienced fighter pilots who were resting after a tour of operational duty. Their task was to pass on the benefits of their experience to the newly-trained pilots.

After being checked out by an instructor in the dual-controlled Master aircraft, I was introduced to the Spitfire. After learning the cockpit layout and all the emergency procedures, I was strapped in and given the all clear to start the engine and taxi out for take-off. The Spitfire is much smaller than the Hurricane, the cockpit is quite cramped and the large nose that houses the Merlin engine restricts the view out. This necessitates a curving approach so that the runway can be seen. In the Hurricane the cockpit is larger and the pilot sits higher and can look forward over the nose.

Once we had got over the first flight each subsequent flight became easier as experience built up. After the first few, which were primarily used to carry out exercises to learn the characteristics of the Spitfire and its various systems, the real training began: formation flying, aerial combat, air-to-air ground gunning and other manoeuvres essential for a successful fighter pilot.

After six weeks at the OTU, the last two of which were spent as a junior instructor, I was sent to the City of Edinburgh Squadron. This was one of the famous Auxiliary Air Force Squadrons that had fought so well in the Battle of Britain. When I joined they were based at Hornchurch, one of the big aerodromes used in the Battle of Britain. Here I was introduced to fighter sweeps across northern France and convoy protection patrols in the southern North Sea and English Channel approaches. Unfortunately, after a month, just as we were beginning to get the feel of front line operational duties, the Squadron was sent to Scotland for less difficult duties.

Life in Scotland was a more relaxed affair. The main task of the Squadron was to patrol the shipping lanes and protect the convoys leaving the Firth of Forth from the threat of German bombers. We had one sighting of these and for the first time I put the safety catch on the trigger to fire the guns. Unfortunately the JU88 which we were chasing dived into the cloud before we could get in range. This was to prove my one and only offensive act in an aeroplane.

After six weeks of enjoying the kind generosity and hospitality of the Scots, I was sent to Benson in Oxfordshire to pick up a new photo-reconnaissance Spitfire and fly it to Cairo in Egypt. The photo-reconnaissance Spitfire had no guns or armour, instead the wings were filled with petrol to enable it to fly long distances and stay in the air for four to five hours, compared with the fighter aircraft which had an endurance of only 1½ hours at the most. My route would take me via Gibraltar and Malta.

I was somewhat devastated by this news. Firstly I had no experience of taking photographs from a Spitfire, and secondly the thought of flying from Cornwall to Gibraltar and thence to

Malta and then Cairo was as good as asking me to fly to the moon. However in the RAF you have to do as you are told, so I reported to Benson to pick up my Spitfire MKIV. I was allocated Spitfire No BP885, and after a few test flights I was cleared to set off on my trip to Cairo.

My first stop was at a small aerodrome in Cornwall called Trebelzue. At the time it was the setting-off point for reinforcement aircraft going to the Middle East, although these aircraft were mostly Wellington bombers with full crews and navigation equipment. I found out at Trebelzue that the Spitfire I was taking was only the fifth to set off en route. I found this out at the navigation briefing just before take-off for Gibraltar.

The briefing officer gave the departing bomber crews substantial information concerning winds at various altitudes, courses to steer and various points on route to make navigation easier for them. I and another officer who was also flying a Mk IV Spitfire to Cairo were the last to be briefed, and the briefing officer admitted that he could not help us very much as we would be flying at 25,000 feet and he had no information on wind speeds at that altitude. He merely suggested a course to steer, giving a warning to keep well clear of the Brest Peninsula and not to fly over Spain. For good measure he advised us to make sure that we fired off the colours of the day when we entered the landing circuit at Gibraltar, as the navy gunners there were likely to think that we were German ME109s, and being trigger-happy would greet us with a salvo, which would not be a pleasant reception.

I am pleased to report that in the event the flight was not too bad. After taking off from Trebelzue in rather nasty weather I broke through the cloud over the Bay of Biscay, and shortly afterwards I could see the north coast of Spain. Being at 25,000 feet I decided to ignore the instructions about flying over Spain but edged towards the Spanish/Portugal border to give myself a better approach to Gibraltar. Without further incident I entered the circuit at Gibraltar, firing off the colours of the day and fervently hoping that the navy gunners would identify me as a friendly aircraft. Thankfully they did and I landed and taxied to a dispersal, where the aircraft was refuelled and serviced ready to take off for Malta the next day.

My night in Gibraltar was a new experience. For a start there was no blackout as in the UK, and the bars and restaurants were filled with soldiers and navy personnel all bent on having a good time. It was fertile ground for the military police, and soldiers and sailors were being marched off to detention centres in substantial numbers to cool off the excesses of drink.

CHAPTER THREE

THE SIEGE OF MALTA

My trip to Malta went off without incident. The weather was fine and I could see the island when I was some 50-60 miles away. It was late afternoon when I arrived over it, and having read of the bombing they had suffered I flew around the island to see for myself the damage that had been inflicted. It was appalling, and I counted myself lucky that I would be away to Cairo the following morning.

Little did I realise the news that awaited me when I landed a few minutes later. Having touched down and taxied to the end of the runway I was met by a corporal on a bicycle. He signalled me to follow him in the aircraft, which I did, and a merry dance he led me. By the time he indicated to me to stop, the engine was at boiling point, and so was my temper. The corporal, having jumped on the wing to help me unstrap, told me the devastating news that the reason he had led me to this seemingly remote spot was that I and the aircraft would be staying on the island, and as from that moment I was a member of 69 squadron.

I subsequently learned that 69 Squadron was a light bomber and reconnaissance squadron flying Maryland aircraft. Their problem was that they had no aircraft; all their Marylands had either been lost in action or damaged beyond repair by the German bombing of Malta.

As I have said, this news devastated me. I realised that I would really be in the thick of the battle for Malta. I found out the following day that there was only one other operational aircraft in the Squadron, and that was another photo-reconnaissance Spitfire like my own. Like me its pilot, Flying Officer Colbeck, had been hijacked along with his aircraft. Colbeck was a New Zealander, and he quickly explained to me our duties, which were to carry out reconnaissance flights over Sicily to photograph the airfields the Germans had built up on the island, and over the large ports in Southern Italy to monitor the movements of the Italian Navy. We also had to search the west coast of Greece and the Tunis peninsula for German convoys carrying troops and reinforcements to North Africa.

During 1940 Italy had reached an agreement with Hitler and had entered the war. In November that year the Italians invaded Greece and moved troops to Abyssinian and Libyan countries which they had captured in the 1930s. This *threatened our position in Egypt and to Greece and our ability to help them fight off the Italians. These efforts met with success. British troops occupied Crete, and in the Western Desert the Italians were routed and many prisoners were taken. However these successes were relatively short lived, and when the German troops arrived to help the Italians the battles along the coast of North Africa surged to and fro and the Germans recaptured Crete.*

To supply the German and Italian troops in North Africa, ships were required to sail from Italian ports across the Mediterranean Sea to Tripoli and other ports along the North African coast. It was in this context that Malta became so important to the Allied cause. Situated just south of Sicily, it was an ideal spot from which to carry out attacks on the Italian convoys taking supplies to the German troops in North Africa. It was also an ideal staging-post for British reinforcement aircraft proceeding to the Middle East.

The British Navy had a strong presence on Malta, mainly submarines; the 10th Flotilla was stationed there. The larger capital ships of the Navy, including the aircraft carrier Illustrious, remained at sea and were serviced from Alexandria in Egypt. It was thought that the risk of bombing by the German Air Force stationed in Sicily was too great.

During the period from 1941 to 1943, the 10th Flotilla of submarines destroyed more than a million tons of German and Italian shipping. Unfortunately they lost 26 submarines in the process. *This harassment of the German convoys, both by the submarines and later by Wellington bombers and Beauforts carrying torpedoes, ensured that none attempted the direct route. Even using the relatively safe routes through the Greek islands, the convoys still incurred losses.*

Colbeck and I in our Spitfires would locate them and report back their position, and that night either the submarines or the Wellingtons would go out to attack them. This caused delays of reinforcements to General Rommel's German and Italian troops by up to five days, something that Rommel could ill afford. As a result the German Air Force attacks on Malta were strengthened and Malta was subjected to some of the most severe bombing ever experienced by any target. The raids started in the latter part of 1941 and their frequency and severity reached their peak in the spring of 1942. These figures give some idea of the pain and suffering the Maltese people endured.

In the first three months of 1942 there were 2,000 raids on the island, more than 20 per day. A thousand tons of bombs were dropped on Malta during February 1942. From February to April more bombs were dropped on Malta than Bomber Command dropped on Germany in the whole of 1942. In March 1942 the number of bombs dropped on Malta was greater than the total dropped on UK cities throughout the war.

All this on a small island less than 20 miles long and 10 miles wide. How the Maltese withstood this battering is almost beyond belief. The award of the George Cross for the islanders' courage, endurance and loyalty was just a small token of the country's esteem.

Throughout this period Colbeck and I carried out our sorties over Sicily and Southern Italy, bringing back vital information on our photos taken with the special cameras installed in the fuselage of our aircraft. When photography was not possible, a visual report was made. By the end of April the Squadron had hijacked two more PRU Spitfires and their pilots, so we had four pilots and aircraft available. This helped to ease the workload.

In 1940 and 1941 the air defence of Malta was carried out by three Gloster Gladiators that had been left on the island by the Royal Navy. As they were in crates, RAF and Royal Navy engineers had to assemble them and make them ready to fly so that they could be used to attack Italian aircraft sent over to bomb the island. They were very successful, and a good many Italian aircraft were shot down. Maltese legend had it that the Gladiators were named Faith, Hope and Charity.

In the latter half of 1941, Hurricane fighter aircraft were flown to the island. They took off from Royal Navy aircraft carriers which steamed under naval escort as far along the Algerian coast as they dared because of the threat of attack by units of the Italian Navy. The Hurricanes were fitted with drop tanks, which gave them sufficient range to reach Malta from their launch point. However at the same time units of the German Air Force were moved to Sicily with orders to eliminate Malta, and by doing so to allow the supply ships ferrying reinforcements to the German Army in North Africa to take the direct route free from the threat of attack from the Royal Navy submarines based on Malta. As a consequence the Hurricanes were confronted with ME109s as soon as they reached the island and suffered severe losses. They were therefore unable to stem the rising level of bombing that had started with the arrival of the Germans in Sicily.

The British Government, aware of the need to keep Malta operational, took the decision to send Spitfires to the island using the same technique that had been used by the Hurricanes. The first of these arrived at the beginning of 1942 and a further attempt was made in March shortly after I had arrived on the island. The number of aircraft on each delivery was 36, but these early attempts met with the same fate as had befallen the Hurricanes. They were attacked by German 109s as they arrived, and shortly after they had landed the German bombers came in to inflict further damage. As a result their numbers were decimated within a few days of their arrival, so the German bombings increased in intensity. Despite these setbacks, the Navy submarines and the Wellington bombers continued their harassment of the German convoys making their way to North Africa, and the damage done to them was considerable.

Colbeck and I played our part in this in that we were flying over Sicily and Southern Italy on a daily basis, keeping watch with our cameras on the movement of German aircraft and shipping. There were several occasions when we could not land at our base aerodrome at Luqa due to German bombing. Sometimes we had to land at one of the other airfields, but on other occasions we would fly south of the island and circle until the bombers had departed.

In April the situation became even worse, in that the ammunition supplies for the Bofors guns used to defend the aerodromes had become so low that the guns were allowed only one clip, that is five shells, per day. In effect this meant that they were almost useless in deterring the 109s from strafing the airfields and other military targets. As a means to boost morale, every member of the armed forces was issued with a rifle with instructions to have a go at the enemy fighters. The chances of actually hitting an aircraft roaring down the runway at 300–400 mph were minimal, but at least it gave everybody a feeling that they were doing their bit.

At this time the effects of the lack of Allied convoys getting through to the island were beginning to be felt. Food was getting scarce, especially for the Maltese people. There was a definite reduction in the amount of food issued to the services, and as far as the Maltese were concerned the attempts at rationing were not very effective. For them it was a case of queuing and scrambling for what was available. With the intensity of the German raids reaching a peak, life for the Maltese was hardly bearable. Even in the Services it was becoming a bit of a strain.

During April it was obvious that something was being planned. Colbeck and I, together with our new colleagues, were doing extra flights to cover the Italian and Sicilian ports to establish the position of the various units of the Italian navy. Further urgency was given to the situation by the fact that our coverage of the Sicilian airfields revealed evidence that the Germans were building glider landing strips at some of the airfields. This could only mean that they were preparing to invade the island. But activity on Malta was also increasing. Large squads of Army personnel were sent to the airfields. Their task was to fill the empty jerry cans which originally contained aircraft fuel with sand. These were then used as building blocks to construct three-sided blast pens which would protect aircraft parked in them from the German raids. This work was proceeding day and night.

There was a persistent rumour that it was all in preparation for a large delivery of Spitfires. This rumour proved correct, and on the 10th May some 60 Spitfires took off from the US carrier Wasp and set off for Malta. The day before this event a Royal Navy cruiser disguised as a merchant ship had crept along the Algerian coast and made a dash for Malta, carrying ammunition and aircraft fuel for the beleaguered island. The ammunition was set up as an anti-aircraft barrage so that when the German aircraft came over to attack and bomb the incoming Spitfires they were met with this surprising barrage of anti-

aircraft fire. This proved a great deterrent against the JU87 dive bombers, and many were shot down.

The Spitfires already on the island had been sent up to meet the incoming German raiders, and they also met with success and shot down many aircraft. Thus the incoming Spitfires from the carrier were able to land safely and were guided to the newly-constructed blast pens, where they were refuelled, rearmed and with a new pilot, made ready to take off and continue the fight against the German ME109s and the attacking bombers.

All this was done in the space of 10–15 minutes. Thus the German raiders were met with a new wave of Spitfires and they suffered heavy losses. From 10th May to 14th May some 100 German aircraft were destroyed, and the battle for air superiority over Malta had been won. There were further raids, but nothing like the severity of those that had been experienced during the first four months of the year.

Malta's problem was now to break the blockade, which was causing shortages of food, fuel and ammunition. The only means of getting these essentials there was by submarine, and the light cruiser such as the one that brought in the supplies immediately before the arrival of the Spitfires on May 10th. This cruiser started a regular run, but in no way could the submarines or the cruiser satisfy the needs of the island.

The service personnel existed on tinned food which had been salvaged from one of the ships which had been sunk in the

March convoy. These were mostly tins of meat and vegetables, and since the labels of the tins had been washed off when the ship sank it was always a surprise to see exactly what the contents were. For the Maltese people, the situation was more serious. They were rationed to 10 ounces of bread per day. This was a basic commodity. Things like sugar, wheat and cooking oil were desperately short and many Maltese had to rely on the soup kitchens that were set up to ensure that they did not starve. The situation was therefore critical.

As a morale booster, King George VI announced that he was pleased to award the Island of Malta and its people the George Cross. This is the highest award for bravery in civilian life and is equal to the Victoria Cross, which is awarded for bravery amongst military personnel. It proved an inspired action, as the Maltese were very proud of their honour and indeed they still are.

At the beginning of June, I and my colleagues in 69 Squadron became very active. Our instructions were to photograph all the Sicilian and Italian airfields and also the naval ports of Naples, Taranto, Brindisi, Messina and Palma. By the 10th June we were covering these targets at least twice a day and sometimes three times. It was obvious that something big was in the offing.

On 12th June we heard officially that two convoys were on their way to Malta, one from Gibraltar and the other from Alexandria. By this time Malta had squadrons of Beauforts and

Beaufighter aircraft ready to attack any enemy shipping. These were in addition to the submarines, so Malta had a significant strike force. The Spitfire squadrons were also carrying out sweeps over Sicily, thus keeping some aircraft on the ground.

Our reconnaissance of the Sicilian ports showed that two large Italian cruisers were in Palma together with their escorting destroyers. On 14th June, the day before the convoys were due to reach the island, I was ordered to make a flight to Palma at last light to make sure that the naval ships were still there. They were still in the same position as established in earlier sorties, but there seemed to be some intense activity around them as if they might be making ready to sail, which in fact they did later that night. However my coverage established their whereabouts and the submarines were alerted to the fact that they looked as though they might sail.

There was worse news to come. The convoy from Alexandria had been forced to turn back. They had come under heavy fire from Italian naval units and had been bombed incessantly by German aircraft based in Crete.

All Malta's hopes rested therefore on the convoy from Gibraltar. Our squadron flew out to find this convoy and had a first sight of it south of Sardinia. It was obvious that it had had a severe battering from the Italian Navy and the German bombers. Of the six ships that had set out, only two could be seen, plus their escorting destroyers. They had been heavily bombed by units of the Italian Navy to the west of Sardinia. As the surviving ships rounded Tunisia, they came under the protecting umbrella first of Beaufighters and then as they got even nearer to Malta, the island's Spitfires. They were able to sail safely into Valetta Harbour, where they quickly unloaded.

This major effort to break the siege of Malta was only partially successful. The tanker that had been part of the convoy was sunk, as three other merchant ships had been, two destroyers and one cruiser. Three destroyers and a minesweeper had been damaged and had returned to Gibraltar. However the island's Spitfires and Beaufighters had shot down 14 German aircraft, and several units of the Italian Navy had been damaged.

The minimal success of the operation did not warrant any letting up of the Island's rationing of food and fuel. If anything, things got worse. There was only one relief, in that the bombing of the island was now very sporadic and mostly confined to quick attacks of fighter bombers. Our reconnaissance of the Sicilian airfields showed that there were fewer German aircraft based there, and we heard later that Hitler had ordered some of his air force based in Sicily to proceed to the Russian front, where the German army was having a difficult time.

Life had therefore become a little less grim on Malta. However, thanks to the shortage of petrol, it was not possible to move freely around the island, so there was little socialising with other squadrons based on other airfields. The shortage of food and drink also made partying a rare pastime. But life was *far from dull, especially at Luqa where our squadron was based. Luqa was the biggest airfield on the island and all the reinforcement aircraft en route for the Middle East used it, so we had many visitors in the mess who kept us in touch with happenings in the UK. They also brought in useful supplies for the bar, so they were very welcome.*

Operationally further reinforcements of Spitfires flew into the island using the aircraft carrier technique that had been successful on previous occasions. Being untroubled by bombing, the strength of the Spitfire squadrons was steadily building up and they were able to take on German raids on an equal footing and not be outnumbered as before. More offensive aircraft were also appearing on the island. Our own squadron had a flight of Baltimores, American light bomber aircraft. Our Spitfire flight had also built up to around ten aircraft.

I had experience of one offensive operation, when I was ordered to accompany a squadron of Beaufort torpedo bombers on an anti-shipping strike just off Pantelleria. The first thing that struck me was how low they were flying. I could see the airstream from their propellers ruffling the surface of the water. I was flying in loose formation on the left of the Beauforts. When we neared the target area the three merchant ships and their two escorting destroyers loomed up ahead, and I was astonished at how large they looked. My previous experience was watching from 25,000 feet when ships, however large, looked small.

The destroyers immediately opened up with anti-aircraft fire and I pulled up to about 8,000 feet to take my photographs of the action. The Beauforts, however, continued in at low level, splitting into two flights that attacked from different directions before loosing their torpedoes at the enemy ships. Once the torpedoes had been released, they turned and began to re-group ready for the flight home.

Fortunately none of the Beauforts was shot down, though several had been hit by the anti-aircraft fire. I took the photos of the attack. One of the ships was burning furiously, while another had obviously been hit and was virtually stopped. The destroyers seemed to be unharmed and were obviously preparing to pick up survivors from the damaged ships. My activities were cut short by the appearance of two ME109s, so I rapidly climbed to a safer altitude and turned for home. An exciting two hours!

In the middle of August we had news that another large convoy was going to attempt to break the siege. Our photographic reconnaissance of Sicily and Southern Italy was stepped up and showed considerable aircraft and naval activity, which clearly indicated that the Germans were aware that a convoy was expected. There were some 15 merchant ships, including the tanker Ohio, in the convoy, and they were heavily escorted by the Royal Navy. This escort comprised three aircraft carriers, one battleship, four cruisers and several destroyers. As soon as the convoy passed through the Straits of Gibraltar it came under fierce attack, first by the U-boats. At this stage one of the aircraft carriers was sunk – a major loss to the navy and to the convoy at such an early stage.

There was a lull in enemy activity until the convoy negotiated the gap between Tunis and the southern tip of Sardinia. Here the convoy was under continuous attack by German aircraft, E-Boats and submarines and units of the Italian navy. Of the 15 merchant ships, only four made it to Malta. The Ohio was abandoned three times by her crew, having been severely bombed and torpedoed, but the captain and crew returned to the ship, and lashed to two destroyers it slowly started to resume its perilous journey to Malta. Thankfully as it passed to the east of Tunis it came under the protection of the Beaufighters from Malta, and as the stricken ship continued slowly east towards Malta the Spitfires maintained a continuous patrol. On the morning of 15th August it sailed into Valetta Harbour, where the ecstatic Maltese were waiting to cheer it in.

The task of unloading the precious oil that it contained started immediately, since the ship was in such a dreadful state that it was barely afloat. In fact shortly after the fuel had been unloaded, the ship broke its back and sank in the harbour. The captain received the George Cross for his gallantry and awards were made to other members of the crew.

So Malta had its fuel, ammunition and food reserves improved, but the cost was horrific: nine merchant ships and their crews sunk, one aircraft carrier, two cruisers, and one destroyer all sunk, and one aircraft carrier, two cruisers and one battleship damaged, some severely. But Malta was still there and still inflicting equal damage to the German convoys trying to get supplies to Rommel, who was still battling it out with the British 8th Army in the Western Desert.

The RAF in Malta were carrying out daily attacks on Sicily with great success, and the Beaufighters continued the good work at night by carrying out intruder patrols. The German shipping losses mounted, and Rommel was beginning to run short of vital supplies.

General Gort felt that conditions had so improved that in September he arranged to hand over the George Cross awarded to the Maltese people by King George VI at an official ceremony in the Palace Square in Valetta. Sir George Borg, the Maltese Chief Justice, received the award on behalf of the Maltese people. The ceremony was watched by some 5,000 citizens, many of whom had walked to the Square, as there was still not enough petrol to run the full bus service. It was a great occasion.

If Rommel was to win his battles in the Western Desert and reach Cairo, his supply routes would have to be reopened. In an effort to do this, the German Air Force started a massive campaign to bomb Malta into submission, and on 11th October three Junkers 88s with a heavy escort of fighters attempted to bomb the island. They were intercepted by Spitfires from 229 squadron and all three bombers were destroyed before they reached the island. The following day eight Junkers 88s escorted by sixty to seventy fighters were intercepted over the sea. Seventy German aircraft were shot down, but some got through and bombs were dropped indiscriminately on Malta. The main formations continued to try and break through the cordon of Spitfires and bomb the island, but very few got through and they suffered high losses. Between 11th and 19th October they had lost 131 aircraft. Only 34 Spitfires were lost. On 20th October the raids ceased.

The breakout from El Alamein also occurred at this time, and as Montgomery's 8th Army fought its way westwards along the North African coast, Malta's long struggle to survive came to a successful end. By Christmas convoys from Egypt were getting through and life in Malta was becoming more tolerable.

During all this time I and my colleagues in 69 Squadron were carrying out photo reconnaissance operations over Sicily, Southern Italy, Greece and North Africa. We were able to bring back photographs showing the disposition of German and Italian aircraft and naval movements. They were invaluable to the High Command planning the defensive, and after 10th May the offensive operations from the island. We were particularly active prior to the delivery of the Spitfires, and during the attempts to get relief convoys through.

To indicate the extent of the change that took place during 1942, it is a fact that when I joined 69 squadron in March we had only two photographic Spitfires in 'A' Flight, 12 Baltimore light bombers in 'B' Flight and eight special duty Wellingtons in 'C' Flight. During this nine-month period I had flown 154 operational trips over enemy territory and 475 hours of operational flying. As a result I was posted to serve as an instructor at a photographic reconnaissance operational training unit in Dyce in Scotland as a rest.

I remained at this unit until October 1943, when I was posted to 682 Photographic Squadron in North Africa. This was a return to operational duties, but the work was quite different. The Allied Forces were now very much on the offensive, and the work of the photographic reconnaissance pilots was to bring back photographs of terrain likely to be used for landing invading troops and of the disposition of enemy forces and equipment.

When the British and American forces had reached Naples, the Squadron moved to San Severo in Southern Italy. From here we covered Munich in South Germany, Vienna in Austria, Pleoic oilfields in Rumania and the west coast of Southern France and the Rhône river right up to Lyon. The work over France was to provide information for planning the landings in Southern France, and to do this we flew from a temporary airfield in Corsica.

During this period the D-Day Landings in Normandy took place, followed by the capture of Rome and Italy and the Allied landings in Southern France. The Germans were very much *on the retreat. Consequently life at the airfield was relatively peaceful. There were few if any raids; our only action was in the air whilst carrying out operational photography. The Germans made frequent attempts to intercept us and shoot us down, but since photographic Spitfires had no guns, if one saw German aircraft climbing to intercept, the policy was to turn and run for home. There was little point in hanging around until the German fighters were close enough to attack, since the chances of escape then would be very slim. It was considered better to bring back some photographs rather than none at all just because we waited too long and suffered the consequences at the hands of fully-armed German fighters.*

Les when he was Managing Director of Hoverlloyd

Leslie in RAF
uniform, 1942

Katie

Les and Katie's
wedding day,
23rd June 1945 in
Ealing, London

Wedding group

Les at Chilbolton, 1948

Leslie in his car

The back of Penn Acres, Chilbolton, family home between 1946-1956

Helen and Jane
Colquhoun,
twins 1949

Helen, Jane and
Peta Colquhoun,
daughters, 1950

Les flew the film can containing the film of the Terence Rattigan
film *The Sound Barrier* (1952) from Blackbushe aerodrome to Belgium,
where it was premièred

Ann Todd with Les in Brussels for the première of the *The Sound Barrier*.
Ann's husband David Lean directed the film.

Invitation to 1953
reunion dinner

GOLDFISH
CLUB

At 14 · SOUTH STREET · PARK LANE · LONDON · W·1

Hon. Secretary:
C. G. LOCKE
78 Morshead Mansions
Maida Vale, W. 9

Chairman:
C. A. ROBERTSON
Vice-Chairman:
W/CDR. R. R. STANFORD TUCK, D.S.O., D.F.C.

Hon. Treasurer:
F. R. STOVIN-BRADFORD
c/o R.A.F. Reserve Club
14 South Street, W. 1

Leslie Colquhoun, Esq.,
"Penn Acres,"
Branksome Hill,
Chilbolton,
Stockbridge, Hants.

18th May, 1953.

Dear Colquhoun,

We are pleased that you are able to come
along to our Reunion Dinner; Invitation Card
enclosed herewith.

As you are probably aware, David Morgan has
promised to attend, Bob Stanford Tuck should be present
and Bill Blunt of "Airmail" will be imbibing with the
rest.

Sir Archibald McIndoe has promised to present
himself at 6-30 sharp "..... in my drinking clothes",
and we are trying to persuade "Bomber" Harris to put
in an appearance.

Yours sincerely,

Hon. Secretary

GOLDFISH CLUB
FOUNDED 1942

SECOND

REUNION DINNER

R.A.F. RESERVE CLUB
14, SOUTH STREET
PARK LANE
LONDON, W.1.

SATURDAY, MAY 30th, 7 p.m.

· 1953 ·

Programme for
reunion dinner

MENU

HORS D'ŒUVRE

·

CONSOMME JULIENNE · SHERRY

·

FILLET OF SOLE BONNE FEMME

·

ROAST DUCKLING   APPLE SAUCE

FRESH PEAS

NEW POTATOES

·

FRUIT SALAD

VANILLA ICE

·

MUSHROOMS ON TOAST

·

COFFEE

TOASTS

H.M. The Queen   C. A. Robertson.

The Goldfish Club
   Proposed by
   Response
Sir Archibald McIndoe,
C.B.E., M.C., F.R.C.S.
C. A. Robertson.

Absent Friends   C. G. Locke.

The Guests
   Proposed by   W/Cdr. R. R. Stanford Tuck,
   Response   D.S.O., D.F.C.
Lt/Cdr. M. Parker, R.N.

Dinghy Drill
   Proposed by   Bernard Wicksteed, D.F.C.
   Response   Major Walter M. Packard,
U.S. Air Force.

Why I am where I am . . . . .
attempted explanation by

Leslie Colquhoun,
G.M., D.F.C., A.F.C.
Test Pilot to Vickers Supermarine.
W/Cdr. P. H. Watts, D.S.O., D.F.C.
R.A.F. Search & Rescue Organisation
David Morgan.
Test Pilot to Vickers Supermarine.
Ex Fleet Air Arm.
Margaret Cornwall.
Only Female Member of Goldfish
Club. Ex-Wren.
S/Ldr. W. A. G. Goldsworthy,
M.B.E.
Hon. Sec. R.A.F. Reserve Club.

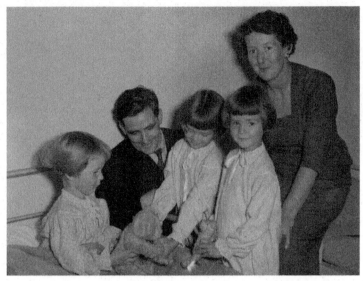

Les and Katie with their three girls. Picture taken for the Evening News, 18th September 1953 before Les flew to Tripoli for the world air speed record attempt

Gathering for the world air speed record attempt

1. **The Plane Arrives**
Lithgow on arrival at Idris Airfield, some 20 miles inland from Tripoli.
He had flown from Chilbolton via Nice and Tunis—flying in formation with Leslie Colquhoun in an
Attacker.

2. **First Welcome**
W/Cdr. Bill Dennis, C.O. of the R.A.F. Station at Idris greets Lithgow.
Idris was formerly known as Castel Benito and is now named after King Idris the First of Libya.

3. **Centre of Interest**
The R.A.F. takes an interest in the Swift—and so do members of the maintenance party. This was the
first time one of Britain's modern fighters had been seen this far afield.

4. **The " Range "**
Part of one ten-mile straight along which the course is marked. The road is one which runs south-west
from Tripoli through Azizia towards the Garian Hills. Montgomery's Army passed this way. The course,
or " the range " as it was known, had already been measured by an Ordnance Survey party, and a three-
kilometre stretch certified as accurate to within ± 3 millimetres.

Part of a booklet produced for the occasion of the record attempt

Measuring devices during attempt to break the air speed record

The record attempt in progress

Air speed record attempt - Mike Lithgow second left, Les third left

Roundabout

The Name's the Same. I'm afraid Leslie Colquhoun (pronounced " Cahoon," as if you didn't know), Supermarine test pilot, has got himself a nickname. While with Mike Lithgow's record-breaking Swift team he was reported in the local North African paper by the name of " Ali El Kahoun."

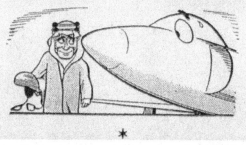

*

Cartoon in connection with the record attempt

Les on the Cresta Run,
March 1954

Les (left) before the run

Les starting
his descent

Presentation for winning the Cresta Run

With his
fellow
competitors

Scimitar taking off at the Vickers airfield in South Marston

Chilbolton test pilots. Left to right: Leslie Colquhoun, Mike Lithgow,
Jeffrey Quill, Guy Morgan and John Derry

Les as chairman of The Spitfire Society with fellow member,
Royston Gumbrell at Hendon Museum

Les (second from right) at the Farnborough Air Show in 1956

Scimitar at South Marston

CHAIRMAN'S COMMENT

CHAIR COMMENT

from Les Colquhoun

I HOPE you are reading this in peace and what goes for quiet these days. Sixty years ago it was a very different story, no peace and plenty of noise of a very different and dangerous character. The battle for Britain was being fought in the skies above and those old enough to be aware of Hitler's threat to dominate Europe, knew he only had to subdue Great Britain to complete that ambition and hoped that the Spitfire and Hurricane pilots would succeed in their defence of this country. They were our last hope.

When our Founder, David Green, conceived the idea of our Society a great number of the original members had fought in that great battle as pilots, or as members of the RAF and the aircraft industry. Sadly, the passing years, seventeen of them, have taken their toll and since those that have survived are in or approaching their eighties this 60th Anniversary of the Battle of Britain could well be he last that is celebrated. That may be so but it would be very sad if it were forgotten. The Battle of Britain is a great milestone in this country's history. Led by the inspirational Winston Churchill the country chose to fight on against the Nazi threat of complete domination of Europe. Thanks to the devotion to duty of those charged with the defence of this country and the ultimate sacrifice of a great many of them Hitler failed to achieve his objective and so enabled this great country of ours to lead the fight back to release our friends on the Continent from Nazi tyranny.

Our Society seeks to perpetuate the spirit that existed sixty years ago not only in the RAF but throughout the whole country. The people of London cheered the visible battles going above their heads despite the destruction of their homes and workplaces by the Luftwaffe bombers. Their courage should also be remembered as well as the stars of the show battling against the odds of more than two to one in the skies above.

The heroics of Dunkirk led me to the RAF recruiting office and there began my career in the RAF. I was sent to Blackpool for my induction in to the RAF leaving my parents to face the dangers of life in London. I felt it was an inspiring period of my life. I had no wish to go to war but it was a necessary fact of life if our country was to be saved from domination.

The unconquerable spirit that pervaded even those who had lost their homes and workplaces and those gallant pilots who day after day fought air battles fraught with danger and risk of death all answered unswervingly Churchill's call to fight "...on the beaches, on the fields and in the streets, we shall never surrender".

That spirit is badly needed now. As new members of the Spitfire Society let us play our part to ensure that the flame of that indomitable spirit lives on . Let this be a call to duty. At the end of our days we can then rightly claim DCO, Duty Carried Out, and sign off.

Cover Picture Details

Superb example of air-to-air photography! Full story on page 29

[Photo: Martin W Bowman]

The Journal of The Spitfire Society

Volume 4 Number 5 Autumn 2000

On the successful completion of every sortie many air forces require their pilots to enter the initials 'D.C.O.' in the Flight Authorisation Book. They stand for 'Duty Carried Out' – a phrase which we think aptly summarises the Spitfire's contribution to world freedom...

Published on behalf of THE SPITFIRE SOCIETY by SPITFIRE ENTERPRISES LIMITED
141 Albert Road South, Southampton SO14 3FR
Tel: 023 8022 7343 Fax: 023 8033 7930
(International Tel: ++ 44 23 8022 7343 Fax: ++ 44 23 8033 7930)

Les's last comment in the DCO, the Spitfire Society magazine

Peta, Leslie, Jane, Katie and
Helen Colquhoun at
Farnborough air show 1956

Sally Colquhoun, daughter 1958

Edith Colquhoun, Leslie's mother, Leslie and Katie outside Buckingham Palace when Les received the George Medal in 1956

Grove House, Blunsdon. Family home 1956-64

Les making a
welcoming speech
at the opening of
the Hoverport at
Pegwell Bay,
Ramsgate

Les test-driving a prototype Vickers hovercraft

Vickers prototype hovercraft fitted out for trials over a wet runway, 1961

VA1 protoype hovercraft ready for trials over water

VA3 prototype preparing for Rhyl to Wallasey service

VA3 Rhyl to Wallasey service

VA3 hovercraft on Rhyl to Wallasey route, 1960

Engineers and staff, Rhyl to Wallasey. Les third from right

Twins Helen and
Jane and sister Peta

Les and Katie with
the three girls

Dinner at the Dorchester, London with fellow test pilots and friends

One of the first Hoverlloyd hovercrafts

Les with Hoverlloyd staff in early days

SRN6 leaving the Goodwin Sands

Cliff Michelmore, centre, waiting to board hovercraft.
Les Colquhoun on the right

Les (centre) with
Sir Christopher
Cockerell in July 1968

The Duke of Edinburgh going for a ride on SRN4 Swift after opening
the Pegwell Bay Hoverport

Hoverlloyd SRN4

Mary Wilson, wife of the prime minister, Harold Wilson, at the naming
ceremony of Swift on 23rd January 1969

Sir Christopher Cockerell, third left, Sheepy Lamb and Les Colquhoun
(fifth left) at the British Hovercraft Corporation

SRN6 coming into Ramsgate Harbour

SRN4 coming onto landing ramp

SRN4 in hangar at Pegwell Bay undergoing maintenance

Aerial view of Pegwell Bay hoverport under construction

Early stages of construction of the hoverport at Pegwell Bay

Aerial view of Pegwell Bay hoverport

Early hovercraft, possibly on the Solent

SRN6 at Calais, Les Colquhoun walking towards the camera

Cars leaving the SRN4 hovercraft

Hydrofoil Brighton Dieppe Service

Sir Robert Menzies, Lord Warden of the Cinque Ports,
at the time of his hovercraft trip

Leslie Colquhoun, third from left at the British Aircraft Corporation 1965

Leslie Colquhoun
before a test flight
of a Swift

Helen, Jane, Peta, Sally, Katie and Leslie 1967 outside Fordyce, Broadstairs

Leslie presents a trophy at the 1952 annual sports day at
Drayton Manor School, his old school

Relaxing in the back garden of Penn Acres with family and friends

CHAPTER FOUR

TEST PILOT

Although there must have been many dangerous moments and narrow squeaks during his time in Malta, Les admits to one incident which upset him, on a flight over Sicily. His squadron had just received a consignment of chocolate, which was considered almost as valuable as gold. Les took a packet with him to eat during the flight.

I was flying over Cape Passero, the south eastern extremity of Sicily, and came down to 16,000 ft to take off my oxygen mask to eat some chocolate before setting course for Malta. Suddenly I saw a shadow and just behind me, almost in formation, was an ME109. His guns must have jammed, or he was out of ammunition, or was a pupil on a training flight, for he did not fire at me, and of course I had no guns. I called up Luqa madly for help, but the 109 flew away and all ended well – for me!

Maybe that was one moment when chocolate did not taste so good.

That incident must have been extremely upsetting, for it seems fairly certain that the ME109's guns had jammed; a German on a training flight would not have been nosing around a Spitfire, nor would he have done so if his ammunition was running low. He obviously had evil intent.

In June 1942, Les had the job of flying around Italian ports, including Naples, Taranto, Messina, Augusta and Palermo, to investigate the disposition of the Italian fleet. Late on the evening of 14th June that year, when the light had faded too much to take photographs, he saw a force of two cruisers and four destroyers steaming out from Palermo. About this time a British convoy was coming through the Mediterranean, heading for Malta. The information Les brought back enabled the necessary action to be taken and one cruiser was subsequently damaged by a British submarine. For this valuable reconnaissance, after months of dangerous unarmed PRU work, he received the DFM. Shortly after this he was commissioned.

During his eight months in Malta he did an enormous amount of flying over enemy territory, land and sea. He logged over 500 hours in that time and thoroughly earned his promotion and decoration. He was in Malta during most of the period when it was in greatest peril from possible assault and during the worst of the bombing.

I remained with 682 Squadron until October 1944 during which time I flew 82 operational trips over enemy territory involving 262 hours of operational flying. Not as arduous as the Malta tour of duty but nevertheless an exciting period at times. For the latter half of the tour I was the Flight Commander and as such was responsible for planning operations, this administrative task reduced the time available for actual flying. During this period I was awarded the Distinguished Flying Cross for outstanding photographic work.

By this time the war against Germany was virtually won, although it wasn't until May 1945 that Germany finally surrendered. During these closing stages of the war I spent part of the time as an instructor at the Photographic Reconnaissance operational training in Dyce.

From Dyce, Les was moved with the squadron to Haverfordwest, and in February 1945, when Jeffrey Quill, chief test pilot of the Supermarine Division of Vickers, wanted another test pilot, Les was sent to join him at High Post in Wiltshire, as his qualifications and temperament were just what Quill wanted. The signal that he had been selected and was to be posted to Supermarines was one of the big moments of his life. He continued as a Flight Lieutenant until April 1946, when he was demobilised. The only difference this made was that one day he arrived for normal work in uniform and the next day in civvies.

Towards the end of the war, Leslie met Kathleen Penty, the youngest of three daughters of Edith and Percy Penty. Edith and Percy's marriage was not a successful liaison and they separated, leaving Edith to bring up the three daughters. They moved to Ealing, London, from Bradford when Kathleen was twelve years old. Leslie and Katie, as she was always known, met through mutual friends at the tennis club.

At this time she was working in a bank in the city and helping at the New Zealand Club during the evening. With the war and Leslie's postings abroad they saw each other infrequently, but there were occasions when Leslie flew a Spitfire home for the weekend, landing at what is now Heathrow. I am not sure if these flights home were acceptable, but he certainly got away with it, and I am sure Katie was more than pleased to see him.

They were married on 23rd June 1946 in Ealing, after Les had taken up his post at High Cliff. They remained very happily married for 55 years. Their first home was a rented house near Salisbury.

At this time they were testing the later models of the Spitfire and it was the test pilot's duty to clear the production aircraft, the main criteria being general handling, stalling and spinning characteristics, high-speed flight characteristics and performance, which included climbs and level speed. In the early days the pilot was responsible for recording data by writing information on a kneepad. This eventually developed into duplicate instruments, and then electronic methods, which were of course far more comprehensive. Other aircraft tested were the Attacker, Swift, Seagull and Scimitar.

Vickers Supermarine moved from High Post to Chilbolton in the early part of 1947. Apart from his work in testing production machines, Les had an interesting diversion when he flew as second pilot on the delivery flight to Buenos Aires of the President's personal Viking. The route took him via Iceland, Greenland, USA, Nassau, Jamaica and Rio.

On August 28th 1948, Les won the Hythe Aero Trophy Challenge at Lympne Airfield, flying the Spitfire Trainer Prototype at 324 mph. This was the last year that this event took place, the two previous winners being William Humble in 1946 and Peter Twiss in 1947. The rather large and impressive cup has been in the family ever since.

At about this time, Les and Katie bought and moved into their first house, Penn Acres, Branksome Avenue, Chilbolton. This would be their home for the next eight years. In 1948, identical twins were born, Helen and Jane. Mike Lithgow wrote about Les' reaction in his book *Mach One*, "The only occasion on which I have seen him slightly shaken was when he became the father of twins".

Eighteen months later a third daughter, Peta, was born. Katie had her hands full, but was helped by Betty Ridout from the village.

While they were at Penn Acres two extensions were built, and part of the house was converted into a village store. This was run by Katie and a friend of hers from Leckford, Marjorie Hayes. They don't appear to have made any money, but they provided a valuable and friendly service to residents of the village. Leslie and Katie both entered fully into village life, becoming parish councillors, and Les played for the village cricket team. Leslie frequently told the story of the time when while changing his trousers he glanced out of the window to see his car rolling backwards down the drive towards the road – needless to say he moved extremely quickly!

There was a lengthy period away starting on 4th October 1950, when Leslie flew an Attacker to Pakistan, making a number of stops on the way. One can only assume there were problems with the aircraft and the Pakistan Government. He left Pakistan on 9th December, arriving back at Chilbolton on the 15th. It was a time when Katie was provided with a Vickers driver to do her weekly shopping; it could not have been easy with three very young children.

One by one aeroplanes were arriving at Chilbolton from various dispersed airfields, so villagers in Chilbolton and nearby Leckford must have been aware that some development was taking place. The test pilot team in those days consisted of many household names in aviation circles: Jeffrey Quill, Mike Lithgow, John Derry, Dave Morgan, 'Chunky' Horne, Peter Robarts and 'Pee Wee' Judge. Les was the only one living in Chilbolton. Tree-lined and unmade, Branksome Avenue contained only three houses and a number of nissen huts, which were later renovated.

Many of the men working on the aeroplanes either bought houses or stayed in lodgings in the village, and with the arrival of Follands, who took over the hangar on the east side of the airfield in the early fifties, the aerial activities must have made an impact on the social and economic activity of the village. Certainly the village pubs must have noticed the change. The jolly parties and convivial evenings at the New Inn, the Seven Stars and the Peat Spade provided many happy memories:

It was after an inter-department cricket match on the airfield. That was a wicket for the brave. I had a reputation as a fast bowler and can remember knocking out the manager of the Vickers' Newbury Works. Fortunately he revived and I was able to buy him a beer afterwards as some recompense.

This may seem a far cry from the activities of the airfield, but it is in fact complementary. Such activities provided relaxation from the business of testing aeroplanes. Test pilots were excellent table tennis players. When not flying we would spend hours playing the game, always for a side stake. Some horrendous sums were involved at times, but by virtue of a double or quits process it is doubtful if much more than a ten-shilling note ever changed hands. The table tennis room was a great place for getting rid of the inhibitions and tensions and it was a great pity when the draughtsmen from Hursley Park moved to Chilbolton and the table tennis room had to be used to house them.

Chilbolton was Vickers Supermarine's experimental airfield, so during the period of Vickers' tenure of the airfield all the company's prototype fighter aircraft were flown and developed there. The process of doing a first flight is a painstakingly careful business. Only on films do you see the debonair pilot leaping into the cockpit and launching forth into the air. The inspection process after the aircraft has been finally assembled can take up to a week. All the systems have to be checked and rechecked and the engines have to be run and tested. Only when the inspectors are absolutely sure that the aircraft is as near perfect as the human hand can make it is it declared ready for flight. The pilot then takes over. He must make sure that all the systems and controls function in the way the designer intended and feel right. Taxi runs down the runway are made at ever-increasing speeds so that the effect of controls can be appreciated before the aircraft actually leaves the ground. This process might take all day, and must be endured. It must be remembered that what is at stake is not just a pilot's life but at least three years of design and development work that has gone into the project, at a cost of many millions of pounds.

Finally the great moment comes. The pilot declares that on this run he will take it into the air. This he does and the aircraft climbs steadily away. On this first flight there is no snappy retraction of the undercarriage as the aircraft leaves the ground; on the contrary, this is left until the aircraft is at a safe height and all the hydraulic systems are brought into use when the UP selection so made can be monitored.

Generally the aircraft disappears from the view of the anxious watchers on the ground. The chief designer is understandably nervous, as also are the other watchers who are generally made up of representatives of those who have designed and built the plane. The sigh of relief when the plane is back in sight is clearly audible and the back-slapping and obvious joy when the aircraft touches down safely is totally genuine and sustained, even when at the subsequent debriefing problems are reported. It is truly a great moment in the life of an aeroplane.

Prototypes operated from Chilbolton were the later marks of the Spitfire and Seafire, notably the MK 24 and the MK 47. Although these aircraft were in fact being tested whilst the unit was still at High Post, the work at Chilbolton was concerned with handling trials with various types of armament and bomb loads.

The Spiteful and Seafang were the RAF and Naval versions of a new breed of piston-engined fighter aircraft. Although some thirty Seafangs and twenty Spitefuls were built, neither aircraft went into service. The principle reason for this was the arrival of the jet engine on the aircraft scene. It is worth noting that Spiteful RB 518 flying from Chilbolton was the fastest piston-engined fighter aircraft in the world.

CHAPTER FIVE

BREAKING THE
SOUND BARRIER

Today supersonic flight is old hat - even the Space Shuttle missions arouse only passing interest. Yet in the late 1940s and early 1950s, such feats were but distant dreams. The potential of the jet engine, providing almost unheard-of power far superior to anything ever foreseen in the conventional combustion engine, was being assessed and was arousing the attention of aircraft designers. Such power could propel aircraft at Mach numbers which were unheard of, in fact Mach numbers were a relatively unknown terminology.

Thus the stage was set for a period of transition in the aircraft industry. Firstly there was the total change from piston-engined power to jet-engined power, and with the power potential on the jet engines being realised, reaching the speed of sound or even breaking through the barrier and achieving supersonic flight was within reach. The second challenge was therefore to achieve that objective, and the period immediately following the end of the war and up until the 1960s saw that transition bearing fruit.

Not however without cost. De Havilland was the first British company to achieve supersonic flight. This was in the DH108 flown by John Derry. John had taken over the development of the DH108 following Geoffrey De Havilland's fatal crash in the first version of the DH108 in 1946. He had been on a test flight to check the high-speed handling characteristics of the DH108 prior to an attempt at the world speed record. Analysis of a recorder fitted to the aircraft showed that prior to breaking up, the aircraft had experienced extremely high reversals of positive and negative G until the aircraft disintegrated.

John Derry, who had just joined De Havilland, was chosen to take over the DH108 development programme, and thus work started on the third prototype DH108. This aircraft had been made stronger than the one that crashed with Geoffrey De Havilland. John Cunningham did the initial testing and then handed it over to Derry. Reading Derry's accounts, the tests that followed are full of drama and at times quite frightening, since at the transonic stage there was virtually no real control over the behaviour of the aircraft. The tests eventually proved that the DH108 could achieve supersonic flight, and are a tribute to John Derry's exceptional ability as a pilot.

Not unnaturally, De Havilland's rivals in the aviation world, Vickers Supermarine and Hawkers, were spurred by news that De Havilland had achieved supersonic flight. The Swift and

Hunter, both Avon-powered swept-wing fighters, were in the initial stages of development. Both were having problems in the transonic range with severe buffeting and lack of elevator control. These problems were due entirely to the fact that neither company had realised that some form of power-operated controls was essential if aircraft were going to fly safely into the supersonic era.

De Havilland, who had the experience with the DH108, had already realised this, and their DH110 had some form of power-assisted control. They had achieved Mach numbers in excess of 1.0 in shallow dives. Hawkers also fitted power-assisted ailerons to the Hunter, and at the Farnborough Air Show in 1952 both John Derry and Neville Duke demonstrated sonic bangs throughout the week. Tragically John Derry and his observer were killed when the DH10 disintegrated in mid-air on the Saturday of the air show. Subsequent investigation showed that some form of structural failure was the cause. It was a devastating day for Les and Katie, as they were good friends of John and his wife Eve.

Vickers, with the Swift, still had spring tab ailerons and could only demonstrate the aircraft subsonically. The aircraft suffered from severe aileron flutter at around Mach .93. Fortunately, although flutter was experienced on most days of the show, the problem stopped when speed was decreased. It is ironic to think that the Swift suffered this very severe phenomenon on a daily basis throughout the show but did not have any structural failure, such as occurred on the DH100. In November the Swift was fitted with its power-operated ailerons and achieved supersonic flight in a steep dive.

Luckily the public enjoyed the sonic bangs. They seemed to feel part of the development process, and if the pilot failed to deliver his sonic bang his demonstration was considered a washout. However, the insurance companies were not so happy, as claims for structural damage to roofs and greenhouses grew rapidly and after 1955 sonic bangs were banned.

Moving on from the supersonic bangs to air speed records, Vickers attempted this in 1953 in North Africa with the Swift MK4:

This unique occasion was marked by my being made an Arab citizen. There is a splendid drawing of me in my robes, done by the famous aviation cartoonist Wren. New name Ali El Kahoun!

The world air speed record has always had a glamorous attraction for designers and for pilots. Substantial prizes were on offer in the early part of the twentieth century to the record breakers, and there can be no doubt that the early development of the aeroplane was accelerated by such activity. Perhaps the most outstanding example was the Schneider Trophy. This event, which was for seaplanes, saw the record increase from 200 mph to 401 mph in the space of four years. This speed was achieved by the Supermarine S6B, designed by R J Mitchell, who later designed the Spitfire. There can be no doubt that the experience gained in the Schneider Trophy was of great value to Mitchell when he came to design the Spitfire.

Preparation for WWII prevented any serious record attempts until after the war, by which time the jet engine was the primary source of power for most aircraft. The RAF high speed flight succeeded in raising the world speed record to 616 mph, in a Gloster Meteor MKIV. At these speeds the effect of compressibility, ie the shock wave which began to build up as the speed of sound was approached, was considerable. The speed of sound is 762 mph at sea level. As this speed is approached a shock wave builds up in front of the wing and drag is increased significantly. This can be overcome by sweeping back the wings, for example with the shock wave on a straight-wing aircraft, eg Meteor, Vampire, Hurricane etc, effects become apparent at a Mach No of .82, ie the speed of the aircraft measured as a percentage of the speed of sound, but by sweeping back the leading edge, Mach numbers of .93 to .97 can be reached. Hence in 1950 the shape of aircraft began to change, and the era of the swept-wing aircraft arrived with the Hunter, Swift and American Sabre.

Shock waves do not just increase drag as air passes over the wing; they also affect the controls. The speed of sound changes with temperature and altitude. The higher the temperature, the higher the speed of sound. Air density, which is much less at 40,000 ft, also has an effect. The pilot's only measurement of speed is by the airspeed indicator, which does not compensate for air density. Consequently an indicated speed of 400 mph at sea level represents a Mach no. of .53, ie 53% of the true speed of sound at 30,000 ft. If the pilot could maintain the same IAS of 400 mph at that altitude, the Mach No would be .97. The Machmeter is therefore an important instrument.

This variation of the speed of sound with temperature and density becomes important when considering attempts on the world air speed records in the 1950s. Because of an unusually cool summer, the Meteor team had to wait a whole year before they could achieve their maximum of 616 mph. When Neville Duke broke the record in July 1953 in the Hawker Hunter, he did so on a course set off the southern coast between Littlehampton and Lee on Solent. Neville Duke's record was 727 mph. For Vickers to beat this it was necessary to make the attempt in a warmer climate. For technical reasons the aircraft could not be released from its ministry contracts until mid-September.

And this is where Les' story begins:

The rules governing a record attempt were laid down by the Federation Aeronautique International and basically said that the record should be the average of four runs up and down a three-kilometre course and the aircraft must be straight and level for one kilometre before entering the course.

At speeds over 700 mph this means very sophisticated measuring equipment, and this has to be approved by the Royal

Aero Club, which acts on behalf of the FAI in this country. Vickers felt that the Swift Mk 4 needed to be fitted with a reheat system, a means of increasing the thrust of the engine by some 20–30% by introducing neat fuel into the jetpipe downstream of the engine, where it is ignited, thus accelerating the speed of the exhaust gases and increasing the power of the engine. Those who have been to Manston will have seen the Tornado and Jaguar jet fighters with a bright glow in the jet pipe as they zoom away. That is the reheat system in operation. You will also have felt a crushing effect of noise. Concorde was the same on take-off.

Vickers' attempt had to be made in an area where higher ambient air temperatures than in the UK were the norm. In theory this would make higher indicated speeds possible and higher Mach numbers. The Mediterranean coast of Libya was considered ideal, so during the first week in September I co-piloted a Valetta aircraft to Idris airport, south of Tripoli, charged with the task of selecting and marking out a course ready for a record attempt later in the month. On board were surveyors, weathermen and electrical experts from RAF Farnborough and members of the Royal Aero Club.

This was considered a highly secret mission, for obvious reasons. It was no easy task finding a course in the middle of the desert, but 50 miles south of Tripoli there was a stretch of road running straight for at least ten miles. The team were taken out to start work on measuring the course and setting up plinths for timing equipment and cameras. There were no facilities on site, just miles of open desert. There was no water and the sand was not suitable for making concrete. Temperatures were over 100 degrees Fahrenheit.

Despite the blistering heat, the surveyors and engineers worked for up to ten hours a day. There was a problem during the first night, as the brass studs let into the road to mark the kilometres were lifted and doubtless sold in the local Arab market. Thereafter studs sunk into the road were covered in Tarmac until required.

Despite the gruelling conditions and hard work, a good time was had by all in the mess. A fine job was achieved, despite the limited time and conditions.

On returning to Vickers, the Swift WK198 was being repainted and prepared, and especially important was the new system for cooling the pilot. This comprised blowing cool air through a specially-designed suit comprising open-ended tubing, so that cold air was blown directly on to the pilot's skin!

On 22nd September, Mike Lithgow and I took off from Chilbolton in the Swift and Attacker to fly to Idris, calling at Nice and Tunis to refuel. On 23rd and 24th September, calibration flights over the course were carried out. On Friday 25th September Mike did four timed runs, setting up a new world record of 735.7 miles per hour. This despite the fact that fuel gauges failed to operate, causing Mike to cut short reheat time.

This failure of the timing equipment prevented any further attempts until the spares arrived. During this period a decision was taken to get the record set on 25th September ratified. This meant that further attempts would have to exceed 745 mph to meet requirements

Mike made some further attempts, but after the first run at 748 mph the reheat failed and the attempt had to be aborted. At this time news arrived that an American Skyray had set up a new record of 765 mph, clearly outside the Swift's capability, so the exercise was abandoned.

Although we returned home with our record already beaten, we had at least accomplished what we had set out to do. Regardless of whether we had broken the record or not, we were anxious to show that the Swift, which was a standard production aircraft with an outstanding range, was not far behind in the matter of performance. It had had no special preparation whatsoever. We were also anxious to obtain some first-hand information on the behaviour of the aircraft under tropical conditions, and the lessons learnt were invaluable.

It was the last time the world air speed record was run in this way, i.e. low level runs over a measured distance. Subsequent attempts were all at high altitude using sophisticated radar techniques.

Supermarine Test Pilot Leslie Colquhoun was flying an Attacker Naval jet fighter at 450 mph when the outer tip of his starboard wing folded up and remained vertical. The ailerons were locked and the controls almost useless. The *London Gazette* of August 1950, under the headline 'When Ordinary People become Heroes', said that Colquhoun, aged 29, ex-RAF ace and already holder of the DFC and DFM, could have pressed the button that would have catapulted him out to a safe parachute landing, but he knew the fault might never be traced if he crashed the jet. At the time of his emergency he was practically over his home, Penn Acres, at Chilbolton, where his family were unaware of what was happening above them.

By using full left rudder he notched his speed up again to over 200 mph and at that speed, twice normal landing speed, he touched down on the mile-long runway at Chilbolton. The plane stopped with only twenty yards of runway left – with nothing more than a burst tyre. For this he was awarded the George Medal. It is thought to be the only medal ever awarded for bravery in Chilbolton skies.

Dennis Webb, author of *Never a Dull Moment* (2001), was outside a hangar at Chilbolton and saw this event. He wrote that the aircraft's starboard outer plane was very slowly waving up and down and had very obviously had come unlocked at the wing fold. He concluded that with the wing partially folded, Les Colquhoun's ailerons were locked and he therefore had no lateral control.

As Dennis drove Colquhoun back to the office he asked 'God Almighty, Les, why didn't you use the ejector seat?' Les replied 'Lord no, Webby! Those things put the fear of God in me!'

That decision saved his life, however, because he was too low to have ejected safely. He also saved his aircraft so that the fault could be found and rectified. This saved Supermarine and the Air Ministry much work and expense.

The George Medal was presented some time later at Buckingham Palace.

Among the many congratulatory letters and sundry telegrams Les received, one was from the Royal Society of St George. In the letter they offered him an Honorary Membership of the Society. The General Secretary went on to say, "The Society, as you can see from the enclosed, is composed of large numbers of those who love England, and we feel that if you accept this invitation you will be doing the Society a great honour".

Soon after this event a film crew invaded the sanctuary of Chilbolton. This was for David Lean's film *The Sound Barrier*. The aircraft which was the star of the film was the Supermarine Type 535 VV119, which for the film was named 'Prometheus'. The film crew took longer than anticipated to finish because of the incessant rain, and were there from the end of 1951 until well into 1952. The film was shot during the day and rushes of it were shown in the nearest cinema, which was in Andover. The Andover people flocked to the cinema to see the day's shooting, which was projected for them to see and comment upon after the main performance had finished.

British Lion, who produced the film, allowed the Royal Air Force to fly a copy of it over to Brussels. On the 13th November 1953 a crowd gathered at Brussels Airport to welcome Les Colquhoun, who flew the 'Prometheus' with a copy of *The*

Sound Barrier. Before landing he carried out a demonstration of the capabilities of the plane. The film was taken to the Palais des Beaux Arts, where it was shown before HRH Prince Albert of Belgium.

From Attackers, Colquhoun went on to test Scimitars. This plane was very successful in service with the Royal Navy. It was the most powerful aircraft flying at the time. Its two Avon engines, developing 2200 lbs of thrust, succeeded in ensuring that the 29,000 lbs of aircraft and equipment became airborne from the aircraft carrier *Ark Royal*. In 1956 production was moved to the Vickers factory at South Marston, just outside Swindon.

Les continued to test the last of the Scimitars from South Marston until 1959. The Duncan Sandys axe had cut off further orders for fighter aircraft for the RAF and the Navy, so Vickers had to diversify their interests. Freeze-dried food was one outlet, and although Colquhoun liked being on the tasting panel it was a far cry from testing fighter aircraft.

Eventually it was necessary for the family to move from Chilbolton to the vicinity of South Marston. As in all domestic matters, Katie took over and started looking at houses. They fell in love with an old farmhouse in Blunsdon, which also had a number of old barns, an orchard and a field.

After the purchase, they realised with a certain amount of horror that there was daylight coming in through the roof. Quite luckily it was summer. Before going off on holiday they had to reroof the building, an expense they could have done without.

Not being very experienced in these matters, they were happy for the builder to take away the Cotswold tiles and replace with slate, something they very much regretted later. Much use was made of the fields and barns and we children took up riding, so horses arrived to keep the grass down.

The fourth and final daughter, Sally, was born on 15th March 1958, sharing a birthday with Leslie. Katie's mother and Leslie's parents moved to houses in Blunsdon from London on their retirement. This time Katie turned part of the house into a hairdressing business, run with a friend from the village, Molly Francis.

It was during this time that Swindon Gliding Club was formed and Leslie became chairman. He was soon flying gliders instead of jet aircraft. The club was very successful and our barns hosted a number of very jolly gliding club parties.

CHAPTER SIX

HOVERCRAFT PIONEER

Returning to the diversification of Vickers, all was not lost. The general manager had heard what Saunders Roe were doing on the Isle of Wight and he contacted the NRDC (National Research and Development Council) and negotiated a deal to give Vickers a licence to develop hovercraft. By the time this had been granted, the SRN1 had started its first trials.

Sheepy Lamb, who was conducting the trials, was like me a test pilot and I knew him well, so after they had completed the Bleriot Anniversary Flight I went to Cowes and had a go on this strange beast. There was no doubt that the transition from land to sea worked exceptionally well, but controllability was definitely lacking. A great deal of anticipation was necessary to ensure that any chosen manoeuvre would be performed safely, but it was great fun. When doing the spinning plate routine, it was quite hilarious. I sometimes wondered what passing boats thought of this strange and noisy beast.

By June 1960 Vickers were building their own. VA1 was quite a different beast. Rectangular not round, two engines not one, one to provide the lift air, the other to provide thrust for propulsion. This was built in conjunction with Hovercraft Development Limited. A Permit to Fly had to be applied for from the Civil Aviation Authority before it could attempt to fly or hover as promised, because they considered that the machine came under the aircraft category.

Les continued to fly this early prototype. Meanwhile another hovercraft, the VA2, capable of carrying four or five people, was under construction but still primarily for trials and demonstrations. It was first flown by Les in the autumn of 1962, and in January 1963 it saw service over snow and ice in England and was taken to the continent in March 1963 for demonstration purposes. In mid-1963 it was modified and fitted with a new type of skirt consisting of an inflatable rubber structure fitted to air nozzles under the craft, which gave it an improvement of about 200% in ground and wave clearance.

The VA2 was exhibited very successfully by Les at the NATO exercise 'Realist' on the River Danube at Ingolstadt, Germany. It returned home via Amsterdam, where it stayed for a couple of weeks and was demonstrated to the press. A notable passenger was Prince Bernhard of the Netherlands, who even took over the controls for a brief time. These two weeks nearly did not happen, as during this period a road fuel tanker went up in flames and with millions of gallons of petroleum in nearby storage tanks it was rather a distracting situation. Everything was however under control, and thankfully, the catastrophe did not happen.

In all there were nine prototype machines on display and demonstrations were carried out in the harbour at Amsterdam. The final day of demonstrations was the 23rd April, when they experienced the strongest winds, which slightly curtailed the flights, as it was considered too rough for the hovercraft to be operated. What they had come out to accomplish had already been successfully carried out.

The VA2 was then packed on board ship again and returned to Vickers at South Marston before proceeding onto more tests and demonstrations.

In July 1962 Les Colquhoun was put in charge of the world's first hovercraft service, between Wallasey and Rhyl. For this service Vickers had produced the VA3 Hovercoach, which was shipped to Birkenhead as deck cargo. This is Les Colquhoun's own story:

This particular story covers the conclusion of the world's first-ever fare-paying passenger hovercraft service, which ran from Wallasey to Rhyl across the Dee estuary in the period July to September 1962. The service was backed by Vickers, British United Airways (Freddie Laker) and BP. Such was the confidence of the three companies that all the planning and setting up of the service was completed some three months before the Vickers Hovercraft VA3, a 36-seat hovercraft, had even commenced its trials.

These trials began in March 1962 at the Vickers airfield at South Marston. When they were completed in May, the VA3 moved to Southampton for its first water trials. The scheduled start for the passenger-carrying operation was July, so the timescale was exceedingly tight. Suffice to say that the trials went as expected and the VA3 was taken by a small coaster to Liverpool, where it was unloaded by crane into the docks. The engines were fired up and the VA3 proceeded to its maintenance base at Rhyl to be prepared for entering service some seven days later.

The VA3 was fired by four Bristol Siddeley Turnmo 603 free turbine engines; two powered the two lift fans and the others the two propulsion propellers. The passenger terminal at Rhyl was on the beach, but at Wallasey things were more difficult as they had to land on a very steep wall. Six return schedules were planned for each day and BUA set up a special booking office for the purpose of ticketing passengers. There was no shortage of these, as the hovercraft was a unique form of transport and everybody was keen to try it.

However, the summer of 1962 was disastrous. There was a persistent north-westerly wind blowing on the shore at both terminals, causing quite steep waves. As a consequence, on only six days was it possible to operate the full schedule, cancellations being caused by sea conditions and maintenance problems. The service carried some 3,600 passengers out of an expected 10,000. It was certainly a very harassing few weeks. By the 14th September we had made 13 engine changes and had reached the situation where there were no more spare parts available. The VA3 had to be left on the open beach at Rhyl as both the lift engines had failed.

It was unfortunate that the spring tides were building up and with the wind still from the NW, the tides were higher than normal. On Friday night, 14th September, the hovercraft was secured by digging an anchor into the sand so that as the tide came in and floated the hovercraft it was safely anchored. No problems were experienced, but on the Friday, one tide nearer the full spring tide, and with the wind a little stronger, the hovercraft broke loose and Ray Old, my second in command, had to start the propulsion engines in order to prevent it from hitting the sea wall.

The forecast for Sunday was for a severe north-westerly gale gusting to force nine. This was grim news, and a second anchor was dug into the sand in an attempt to secure the craft. At about 7 pm I boarded the VA3 to maintain a watch throughout the night. With me were Ray Old and a cruise line officer, Captain Banbury, who had been seconded to the trials for experience. The wind was blowing a gale and the incoming waves looked ominous. Soon they were lashing the VA3 and as the waves passed under the craft it was lifted up, only to be bounced back onto the sand, followed by the next wave, which would burst over the cockpit and superstructure. All this was very frightening and very unpleasant.

I was in the captain's seat and Ray Old and Captain Banbury were monitoring the passenger cabin, keeping an eye on the structure. The noise was horrendous and it was now dark and lashing down with rain, not that that was important, as there was more than enough sea water, which by now, with the VA3 floating on the end of the anchor chains, was smashing onto the windscreen.

Suddenly there was a tremendous crash, and the nose of the VA3 swung round violently and we were off towards the sea wall. I hastily started up the two propulsion engines and was able to steer the hovercraft away from the wall and out to deeper water. We had broken loose, but had no idea why. It was later discovered that the whole anchor fitting in the bow had been torn out. From the passenger cabin Ray Old reported that the lining amidships and on the sides and ceiling of the hovercraft had been torn apart, indicating substantial bending movements in the structure. In the confusion we could not establish whether or not the main structure had failed, but I was sufficiently alarmed to ask the lifeboat crew who were standing by to launch their boat and come alongside.

By this time the tide was at its maximum height and was running across the promenade. The risks involved in launching the Rhyl lifeboat were indicated by the fact that the coxswain,

Mr Harold Campini, was awarded the Silver Medal for his efforts that night. A commemorative plaque is now displayed on the wall for all to see. This is the only known occasion when a lifeboat was launched to rescue a hovercraft.

With the lifeboat launched, I considered the situation. Ray Old was still doubtful about the cabin structure, and to add to the problems Captain Banbury was very sick. Fearing that the VA3 could break in two, I requested the lifeboat to come alongside and take us off. However, there was no way the lifeboat could come alongside with the propellers whirling around, so the engines had to be stopped, where upon the VA3 swung round beam onto the sea, which added to the difficulty of the lifeboat coming alongside. In fact with the sea running it was impossible.

I had to restart the propulsion engines, pull away from the sea wall again and review the situation. During all of this fracas I had told Ray Old and Captain Banbury to inflate their Mae Wests [life preservers]. I inflated mine, only to find that I was jammed between the back of the seat and the control column. I had to deflate my Mae West, and cursed my stupidity in inflating it in the first place. However it was agreed that the lifeboat would be just astern of the starboard side of the VA3. I would then stop the starboard engine and keep the craft into wind using the port engine.

When the lifeboat crew reported that Old and Banbury were safely in the lifeboat, I stopped the port engine and scrambled out of the cockpit through the passenger cabin and out on the deck, where the brave men in the lifeboat were ready and waiting for me to jump in. Safely in the cabin, I was relieved to gulp down the traditional tot of rum.

So ended a brave enterprise. The VA3, left to its own devices, went alongside the seawall under the influence of the now ebbing tide and some of the engineers jumped on and secured ropes to the engine support struts and lashed the other end to the railing of Rhyl's West Promenade. In the event this was most fortunate, since a couple of heavy cranes were able to lift the VA3 onto the promenade the following morning. It was then dismantled and returned to the Vickers factory at South Marston. Here it was completely reconditioned, including any repairs found necessary, and it then had a series of trials before it was classified as fit for service. Six months later it was operating with the US Marines at Long Island USA.

Fifty years later there are discussions about bringing the service back. With bigger and more reliable craft it could be successful.

As a family we spent the summer in rented properties in Prestatyn. It was a wet and windy period, but we had the opportunity of exploring parts of and North Wales, and Liverpool.

CHAPTER SEVEN

CROSS-CHANNEL ADVENTURES

In 1963 Les was charged with taking the prime minister of Western Australia on the craft, such was worldwide interest. He also spent a number of weeks in Sweden exploring possible sites for hovercraft travel.

1963 also proved to be a sad time. Mike Lithgow, his good friend and fellow test pilot was killed on 22nd October whilst test-flying the prototype BAC One Eleven from Wisley Airfield. When doing stall tests the aircraft entered a deep stall and crashed near Chicklade, Wiltshire. Six other BAC flight test team members were also killed. This had a profound effect on Les, and I think I can honestly say he did not pilot another aircraft.

In November 1963 he flew to Libya via a stopover in Malta. In Libya they carried out hovercraft trials in the desert. Much of 1964 was spent in Southampton, and in June 4th 1964 Les and Katie attended the film première of *633 Squadron*.

Back at the South Marston base, trials of the VA3 continued. In January 1965 the craft was skimming over the ice-laden water of Long Island Sound to New London, demonstrating to the US Navy what could be achieved.

1965 was the beginning of the cross-channel era. Swedish Lloyd and Swedish American Line formed Hoverlloyd to run a service across the English Channel, which then, as now, was one of the busiest sea crossings in the world. After responding to an advertisement, Les was appointed Chief of Operations.

His last day at Vickers was 23rd December. The family moved once more from the countryside of Wiltshire to the east coast of Kent. Whilst Les was fully occupied, Katie dealt with the move and all it entailed. We children, who were still in education, needed schools and each of us had different needs, but eventually this was achieved and we settled happily in Fordyce on the North Foreland Estate in Broadstairs. Shortly afterwards all the grandparents followed.

Dover was considered by the Swedes to be too busy, so a base was built in Ramsgate Harbour. The two SRN6 craft for Hoverlloyd's initial pilot operation were delivered in early 1966. At the same time, the four experienced SRN6 pilots from the now defunct Clyde Hover Ferries were joined by three new recruits. Emrys Jones, also from Vickers, was Chief Engineer.

Before any service could commence, Les and Emrys had the task of obtaining the Permit to Fly and the necessary training of the pilots. Les organised the first hovercraft commanders' training course at Cowes, I.O.W, and Ramsgate during March 1966.

A special pad inside Ramsgate Harbour had been built as the operating base, and at Calais a hard standing was put down to the west side just inside the harbour entrance. The craft were designed to carry 36 passengers. The first scheduled service to Calais commenced on 30th April 1966. Earlier in the month a publicity run was made by both craft to the new Calais Hoverport, carrying 70 VIPs and the press. The weather was not ideal - the sea was rough on the outward journey, though relatively smooth on the homeward one. But after a very good lunch in Calais the reports were very favourable, so for the following two years the two craft, named *Swift* and *Sure*, made regular trips across the Channel, weather permitting.

If the weather was unsuitable for cross-Channel operations, trips to the Goodwin Sands were made when possible, or simply pleasure trips along the coast. If the weather deteriorated while the craft was in Calais, alternative ways of getting back to Ramsgate had to be found, usually by ferry. I can remember more than one trip when as members of the family we had to come back on the craft in horrendous seas, when all around would be a wall of sea! The service was a popular draw for both holiday makers and locals.

These were pioneering days, and amongst the staff there was great camaraderie. Les did not let things go unnoticed and all the milestones were celebrated with parties. Fordyce played host to many happy and riotous evenings.

Les and Katie certainly knew how to throw a party, and all

employees were made welcome. On one such occasion the commanders returned to the house at 12.30 pm the following day to finish off the beer. They eventually left at 6 pm!

In December 1966 Les was made managing director of Hoverlloyd. In 1967 and 1968 he was the key figure in a planning application for a new purpose-built hovercraft terminal or 'hoverport' at Pegwell Bay, just outside Ramsgate, somewhere where the SRN4 could operate. It was a foregone conclusion that there would be objections. Although Pegwell Bay is perhaps not the most scenic part of the coastline, it was well known as a bird sanctuary and attracted many birdwatchers. It was also a popular place for bait diggers, who at low tide dug out lugworms, which they sold on to fishermen. The fishermen and the local residents naturally did not want a busy hoverport on their patch. It was clear that there would be a public inquiry to hear all sides of the argument.

The first inquiry took place in Albion House in Ramsgate and lasted seven days, from 3rd to 12th January 1967. Les was cross-examined for two and a half hours.
Surprisingly Kent County Council was one of the main objectors, arguing that the cross-channel traffic should be concentrated in one place, ie Dover.

The second inquiry lasted three and a half days, from 12th to 15th September. Les Colquhoun, now Hoverlloyd's Managing Director, had this to say:

"If the planning permission applied for was refused, then a

death-blow would be struck, not only for Hoverlloyd, but also for the British hovercraft industry. If this did happen Hoverlloyd reserved the right to reconsider its position. It would be better to break their contract with the British Hovercraft Corporation and pay damages thereby incurred than to embark upon an operation which for them would be commercially unacceptable."

According to the book *On a Cushion of Air,* by Robin Paine and Roger Symes, Tony Brindle, speaking on behalf of the British Rail operation from Dover, said: "Les Colquhoun and I had a very friendly relationship and when it came to the final inquiry at Pegwell Bay, about Pegwell Bay, I was asked to appear. I went and was asked, 'Do you have an objection?' and I said, 'No, I have no objection at all. My job is to see that hovercraft are developing.' If an operator wants to come and take a chance at Pegwell Bay, that is a commercial decision but that was fatal as far as Dr Sydney Jones, chairman of Seaspeed, and I were concerned, because he wanted me to see Hoverlloyd off the premises and didn't care how. He just made life absolutely impossible, but once the decision had been made about Pegwell Bay there was nothing he could do."

The important issue at the time was that the battle for Pegwell was over and Hoverlloyd had won, but Seaspeed had also got what they wanted. Now the battle for the cross-channel hovercraft market was to commence, a battle which sadly, for all their commitment and demonstrable superiority and through no fault of their own, Hoverlloyd would eventually lose.

After this second inquiry Hoverlloyd were granted permission to build the hoverport at Pegwell. Building work commenced in July 1968. Work continued on the SRN4s, which were of the 'Mountbatten' Class. Designed for all-year-round services on open coastal waters with waves up to eight to twelve feet high, they weighed 165 tons and carried 174 passengers and 34 cars, or 254 passengers and 30 cars.

Construction of the new hoverport went ahead at full speed. In sixteen weeks 300,000 tons of colliery shale was brought from the local mines to the site in a fleet of 100 lorries. As much as 5,000 tons a day was unloaded to provide the base for the terminal.

On these foundations three main buildings were assembled: a vehicle examination hall, a maintenance workshop and a passenger terminal, including concourse and offices. The total cost of the buildings and facilities was about £1.5 million. It was officially opened by the Duke of Edinburgh on 2nd May 1969, when the assembled party drank to the health of their guest and the future of Hoverlloyd with four dozen bottles of champagne.

At Pegwell Bay the new SRN4 began trials in January 1969, and on the 23rd it was named *Swift* by Mrs Mary Wilson, wife of the Prime Minister. The climax to all the endeavours came on 2nd April, when the first scheduled service departed for Calais, where the new hoverport, built at a cost of £800,000, had been opened the previous day. A second hovercraft, the *Sure*, was delivered shortly afterwards and named by Mrs Mary Soames, the wife of the British Ambassador to Paris, on 3rd June. The names *Swift* and *Sure* were carried forward from the SRN6s which operated from the harbour at Ramsgate.

After the start in April 1969 the traffic grew rapidly and, although there was competition from Seaspeed at Dover, a load factor of 70–75% was achieved. By 1974 one in every eight cars crossing the English Channel was passing through Pegwell Bay. Talks with Seaspeed had commenced the previous year, and Hoverlloyd, unlike its competitor, was making a profit.

A third hovercraft, the *Sir Christopher*, went into service at the end of June 1972, named by Mrs Cockerell, wife of the inventor. As lack of capacity was becoming a problem at peak periods, a decision was taken to exploit the interior space more effectively and modify all three craft as soon as possible. The Mk.1 version had an interior cabin at car deck level, giving no external view, and passengers frequently felt unwell. This was removed to allow more cars to be carried, and at the same time the outer cabin walls were moved to the edge of the craft. The carrying capacity of the Mk.2 version was increased from 250 to 288 passengers and 30 to 37 cars. All were modified by the end of 1973.

As the Hoverlloyd summer timetable now offered half-hourly departures between 0600 and 2000 hours, almost 60 crossings a day were being made and about 200 a week outward to Calais. To cope with the increased capacity more crew members were recruited.

We cannot leave Hoverlloyd without reading about some of the early adventures.

On 29th November a hovercraft lost a propeller at Ramsgate, causing damage to the terminal building. As a result all craft were grounded pending an investigation, including those at Dover, but they were back in service a few days later. At 19 feet the propellers were the largest of their kind.

On another occasion, in November 1971, *Swift* left Calais in gale force winds. The weather was not unduly severe, and she had made the crossing from Pegwell Bay without difficulty, but a large piece of skirt was torn off and carried away about five miles out. Unable to return to the hoverport, the captain sought a suitable alternative place to land. Fortunately the wide flat beaches from Sangatte to Cap Blanc Nez were available. The *Swift* beached in shallow water, where most of the 145 passengers were able to scramble ashore, their injuries limited to seasickness and wet feet. Much sand had to be dug away before a temporary repair could be effected.

A similar drama occurred in April 1972. Experiencing bad Easter weather, the *Sure* suffered a torn skirt while crossing from Pegwell Bay to Calais. This time the captain was unable to limp back to the hoverport and beached the craft a short distance away. Her almost full load of passengers, cars, caravans and coaches was all transferred directly to *Swift* via the bow ramps to minimise inconvenience. The second hovercraft then took everyone uneventfully to Calais.

In order to improve the level of comfort in bad weather, the captain could choose his course to avoid the worst of the sea conditions. One possibility was to travel over as much of the Goodwin Sands as possible. This new form of transport was able to profit from this previously disastrous offshore shipping hazard to obtain a smooth passage as far as the South Foreland. Care was needed at the southern end, for the sands shelve steeply on the offshore side. A suitable place for departure had to be chosen that did not result in the craft taking a dive into very rough water – not a comfortable experience for passengers and crew.

Hoverlloyd did have a tradition of running charter trips to the Goodwin Sands, even organising cricket matches when the tide was out.

CHAPTER EIGHT

ASHORE AT LAST

In 1973 Les Colquhoun retired. His legacy was Hoverlloyd; he had overseen its development from the very beginning, with a clear vision of what was needed and the determination to make it happen. It became an enterprise to be intensely proud of, producing a highly-motivated workforce achieving a level of dedication and a standard of presentation second to none, and it can be attributed to one man.

The whole time Les was at Hoverlloyd, the service was his priority. First thing in the morning he would check the shipping news, and he would not switch off until all craft were safely back at base. Many holidays and weekends were interrupted by some complication, but he lived and breathed hovercrafts. It was a sad day when he left. The budget deficit undoubtedly led to his departure. Nonetheless, despite the heavy price paid, Les Colquhoun's bold and courageous vision was eventually justified. Hoverlloyd could not have expanded and prospered through the ensuing years without his early determination to get things working in the right direction. He was definitely a people person, and gathered around him a team of dedicated and happy staff. Soon after Hoverlloyd was subsumed by Seaspeed at Dover.

In 1972 Les started his own consultancy business for high-speed marine craft. He also worked with Bell and Rhor of America on surface effect ships in the USA. He later became involved with the London Hovercraft Service which ran between Greenwich and Westminster, using a Vosper side-wall hovercraft.

In 1978 Les joined Jetlink Ferries and ran a Brighton-Dieppe Boeing Jetfoil service sponsored by Associated Newspaper Group, but striking French fisherman blocking the port of Dieppe and withdrawal of sponsorship caused this company to close in 1981.

After all these setbacks, at the relatively early age of 61, Les decided to step away from business and pursue something completely different. In 1982 Les and Katie took over as custodians of Chiddingstone Castle. Having decided that they would like to work together they answered an advertisement in *The Lady* magazine. They were interviewed by the two elderly sisters who were trustees. One was a senior partner in a Harley Street practice of solicitors. They were then offered the job of junior custodians with a token salary; the bonus was living in a castle surrounded by some of the most beautiful Kent countryside. It was all very idyllic.

The accommodation on the upper floor was vast, if somewhat dated. It proved a logistical nightmare for the removal men to move the furniture to this apartment, made worse for having to negotiate their way around the array of basins and tins left out to collect water from the leaking roof. The custodians in charge were very helpful and did everything they could to get Les and Katie settled in.

The village of Chiddingstone is owned by the National Trust, but the Trust did not wish to take over the castle, which was run by a private trust set up for the purpose. In fact it is not a castle but a red brick mansion dating back to the 15th-16th century. It belonged to the Streatfield family who were wealthy iron founders. In the late 1700 Henry Streatfield decided to go upmarket and transform the mansion into a castle. This proved to be a costly business, and rumour has it that he borrowed money from the Earl of Leicester, who lived at nearby Penshurst Place, as a dowry for persuading one of Streatfield's sons to marry the Earl's illegitimate daughter!

The gardens were altered from a formal layout to Capability Brown style, and many trees were planted and a lake created.

The fortunes of the Streatfield family continued to decline. The castle was let out from 1900 and in 1930 the whole estate was sold. During the Second World War the army occupied the building and severe damage was done to it. After the war it became a co-educational school, which of course was frowned on by the villagers. Les and Katie met several old pupils during their stay there.

Scandal eventually caused the school to close some time in

the early 1950s, and in 1955 the property was bought by Denys Bower, a Derbyshire-born collector of some repute. Most of his early life he had been a bank clerk, but such was his passion and taste for antiques that he spent every penny he saved buying and selling. His collection of Japanese lacquer and armour is the finest outside the Victorian and Albert Museum, and his Stuart and Jacobite collections are among the finest in the country. Prior to buying Chiddingstone he had a gallery in Portman Square, which had to make way for a hotel.

Bowyer, despite being an avid collector, was an eccentric. The occasional trespasser was surprised by a shotgun being fired overhead. Stories of weekend orgies and jazz sessions were not uncommon. Worse, he was given a 10-year sentence for attempting to murder his girlfriend. This resulted in problems with looking after the collection and the repayment of loans. The bank asked their solicitors, who happened to be the Harley Street firm which employed the partner who became Chairman of the Trustees. Miss Eldridge went to see Bower at Wormwood Scrubs, and it would seem she fell under his spell, as did her sister. She arranged for parts of the castle to be rented out and began a battle to get Bower released. This she succeeded in doing after six years, and she carried out a cloak-and-dagger game with the press when she took Bower from the Scrubs to her flat in London. She told this to Les and Katie over dinner one evening in their flat.

Unfortunately Bower died not long afterwards, of

pneumonia. Denys Bower's bequest was to form a charitable trust to show the Bower collection to the general public.

It was not an easy few years for Les and Katie, but they worked hard and made a number of improvements, especially around the garden. They did a lot of painting, cleaning and tidying. The flat and castle were cold. One winter Les had to shovel snow off the roof to prevent flooding. At 90 feet above ground with only a small parapet to prevent falling, this was not for the faint hearted.

Finally Les and Katie became head custodians. On taking over the accounts, they realised that the books were in a hopeless state. To help make ends meet the prices of the fishing rights were increased and Katie ran a tea room, which in the first full year made £5,000. Home-made cakes were made by a friend, and it was not unusual to defrost by using the hair dryer.

It was a wonderful place for the grandchildren to visit. There were five of them at this time and they had some exciting times playing in the grounds, in the caves and around the lake.

Having worked extremely hard trying to get Chiddingstone on a more viable footing, Les and Katie returned to Broadstairs for a more relaxing way of life, but not for long. In 1984 Les joined the newly-formed Spitfire Society and became Chairman of the Southern Region, then Executive Committee Vice Chairman and finally Chairman, a post he held until he died in April 2001. The society kept him very busy, too busy Katie sometimes thought, with meetings, talks, mailings, manning stands at air shows, writing articles and generally keeping a large and diverse society ticking along. *The DCO*, the Spitfire Society magazine, described him after his death as a modest, caring but determined man, with a keen sense of humour. He was a considerable asset to the society and would be missed.

In November 1999, one of my brother-in-laws, Chris Storrar, had work connections in Malta and took Les back to the island. Among the many places he visited was the Malta Aviation Museum, where he was warmly welcomed. The museum features examples of aircraft that had a direct connection with the history of aviation in Malta, and must have brought back many memories. Soon afterwards Les' health deteriorated, after which he would have been unable to make the trip.

Les did not often write about himself, but he did so on one occasion. The following article was published in the Southern Region Newsletter of the Spitfire Society, October 1995.

Six Minutes to Burn

Sitting on the runway, Avon engine idling, waiting for control to signal take-off clearance, looking to the immediate left the gaily coloured tented colony of the trade stands, one can almost sense the gin fumes and the smell of rich food. Further down the runway the tightly-packed general public are all anxious to get a good view and enjoy the thrill of the show. Perhaps their nerves are as taut as my own.

The adrenaline surges as the radio crackles the message to get started. Slowly the throttle is opened and through the gate, a tense moment waiting for the reheat to fire up. Release the brakes and Swift Mk3 WK195 accelerates down the runway, 30, 50, 100, 150 knots, lift off and select wheels up holding the aircraft close to the ground, 200, 250, passing the end of the runway still accelerating, pull aircraft up into steep climbing turn on to a heading 45 to right of runway heading. Quick check on instruments, jet pipe temperature, reheat still on, climbing now very fast, 10,000ft, 15,000, 20,000, 30,000, 33,000, 3 minutes since take off, level off into a diving turn to the left on to reciprocal heading of the runway. Airfield in sight almost immediately below. Still on reheat and full throttle, speed accelerating rapidly in steepening dive towards runway, Mach no. .9, .92, .93, aircraft trim nose down of its own accord into even steeper dive, .96, .98, Mach 1, height now 27,000 feet, Mach 1.2 height now 23,000 feet, aircraft in near vertical dive and literally out of control.

Throttle back engine, pull back hard on control column, Mach nos. beginning to fall, .96, .94, control surfaces now becoming effective, adjust aircraft alignment with the 5,000ft runway just ahead, Mach no. .93, ASI 630 knots. Bank on reheat and hurtle down the runway 670 knots and 300 feet. With luck sonic boom will have preceded aircraft by a matter of seconds. End of runway, pull up into near vertical climb, reheat still on, vertical climbing roll left, then right, now at

13,000 feet half roll on to back throttle back and pull through bottom half of loop, adjust speed by use of air brakes ready for second pass down the runway at 550 knots. Eight point roll down, followed by fast roll left. At end of runway pull aircraft into tight right turn trough about 90 degrees execute a John Derry turn which means rolling right into a turn but stopping the roll after 180 degrees, by which time the aircraft is into a left hand turn back towards the runway. Pulling about 5-6g let speed fall off to about 150 knots, lower the undercarriage, lower flaps and carry out slow fly past down the runway.

Once past the stands up with the wheels and flaps, open the throttle, put the reheat on and as the aircraft accelerates away pull a 6g, 180 degree turn for a fast fly past down the runway at 600 knots, fast roll left, fast roll right, and during this manoeuvre pull aircraft into a climbing turn, reduce power and let speed fall off. Call Tower, "Swift downwind", lower undercarriage, lower flaps and as next aircraft takes off touch down on runway seven minutes after take-off. Taxi back to dispersal, the happy and excited faces of the ground crew say it all and one can give a sigh of relief that is over for another day. Thank the ground crew and wander back to the pilot's tent to compare notes.

One ironic thought crosses my mind, I might have broken the sound barrier but no doubt I have broken somebody's window or brought their ceiling down and given sundry people around Farnborough a nasty fright. Thankfully, other people are responsible for dealing with these problems. For the moment I can unwind and relax.

But relaxing was not something that came naturally to Les. Right up until his last few weeks in hospital he was working on various Spitfire Society projects. He was in much demand for talks and presentations, both locally and further afield. He became involved with the local church, serving on the parochial church council for a number of years. In between times he enjoyed time with all his family and grandchildren and there were many memorable family get-togethers.

A bi-annual reunion for test pilots was started at Popham Airfield by Dick Richards. Les enjoyed these occasions very much, as it was a chance to meet up with old friends and talk about the old times. Neville Duke and his wife always arrived by plane, and weather permitting there was an air display by the Spitfire and Hurricane.

Leslie died on 26th April 2001. Following a private cremation there was a memorial service at St Peter's Church, Broadstairs. As mourners entered the church a lone Spitfire flew overhead.

Printed by Printforce, United Kingdom